HOCKEY'S YOUNG SUPERSTARS

HOCKEY'S YOUNG SUPERSTARS

The 25 Hottest Stars on Ice

JEFF RUD

RAINCOAST BOOKS
Vancouver

For Matt, a young superstar in our household

Raincoast Books gratefully acknowledges the ongoing support of the Canada Council for the Arts; the British Columbia Arts Council; and the Government of Canada through the Department of Canadian Heritage Book Publishing Industry Development Program (BPIDP).

Raincoast Books
9050 Shaughnessy Street
Vancouver, British Columbia
Canada V6P 6E5
www.raincoast.com

In the United States:
Publishers Group West
1700 Fourth Street
Berkeley, California
USA 94710

Design by Teresa Bubela
Front cover design by Ingrid Paulson
Photo credits on page 158

Library of Congress Number: 2003092553

National Library of Canada Cataloguing in Publication Data

Rud, Jeff, 1960-
Hockey's young superstars: the 25 hottest players on ice / Jeff Rud.

ISBN 1-55192-637-7

1. Hockey players—Biography. 2. National Hockey League—Biography.
I. Title.
GV848.5.A1R82 2003 796.962'64'0922 C2003-910390-0

Printed and bound in Canada.

10 9 8 7 6 5 4 3 2 1

CONTENTS

Foreword by Chris Cuthbert . . . 7

PROFILES

NIK ANTROPOV, Toronto Maple Leafs . . . 11
DAN BLACKBURN, New York Rangers . . . 17
JAY BOUWMEESTER, Florida Panthers . . . 23
ERIC BREWER, Edmonton Oilers . . . 29
DANIEL BRIERE, Buffalo Sabres . . . 35
MIKE COMRIE, Edmonton Oilers . . . 39
MARIAN GABORIK, Minnesota Wild . . . 47
SIMON GAGNE, Philadelphia Flyers . . . 53
MARTIN HAVLAT, Ottawa Senators . . . 59
DANY HEATLEY, Atlanta Thrashers . . . 63
MARIAN HOSSA, Ottawa Senators . . . 71
JAROME IGINLA, Calgary Flames . . . 77
OLLI JOKINEN, Florida Panthers . . . 85
ILYA KOVALCHUK, Atlanta Thrashers . . . 91
VINCENT LECAVALIER, Tampa Bay Lightning . . . 99
ROBERTO LUONGO, Florida Panthers . . . 105
ANDREI MARKOV, Montreal Canadiens . . . 111
PATRICK MARLEAU, San Jose Sharks . . . 115
DEREK MORRIS, Colorado Avalanche . . . 121
RICK NASH, Columbus Blue Jackets . . . 127
BRAD RICHARDS, Tampa Bay Lightning . . . 133
DANIEL AND HENRIK SEDIN, Vancouver Canucks . . . 139
MARCO STURM, San Jose Sharks . . . 147
JOE THORNTON, Boston Bruins . . . 151

Acknowledgements . . . 159

FOREWORD

Ray Bourque's winning goal in 1996 before an adoring throng in Boston; Dominik Hasek's uncanny foreshadowing of the Nagano Olympics, with his shootout shutout at the 1998 skills competition; Wayne Gretzky's MVP performance in his final All-Star appearance in 1999 — these rank among the most memorable, defining moments of National Hockey League All-Star weekends from the '90s. In each case, a legendary player raised his performance beyond that of an imposing cast of stars to make an indelible mark.

At the 2002 All-Star weekend in Los Angeles, yet another magical performance was forged, on Staples Center ice in the newly minted Young Guns' game. Hockey's preeminent entry-level players had been summoned to Hollywood for a casting call, to provide a warm-up act for the All-Star Game's feature presentation. Ilya Kovalchuk and teammate Dany Heatley, Atlanta's "Goal Dust Twins," headlined hockey's version of the brat pack, a group eager to steal some notice.

"It was a competitive atmosphere," remembers Edmonton Oilers' centre Mike Comrie. "Everybody was anxious to make their mark."

Comrie wasted little time, scoring his first of three goals before the game's two-minute mark. Heatley hit the scoresheet next in the four-on-four action, before Kovalchuk began to put his stamp on the proceedings. The Russian sniper fired a natural hat trick in the first period and he was just warming up.

"Hey, Heater, how do you get that guy off the ice?" Team Melrose coach Barry Melrose yelled in jest to Heatley about his linemate overstaying shifts. Kovalchuk didn't come off until he had scored six times that night, the difference in a 13-7 victory for Team Melrose. His "six-shooter" performance was a warning shot over the NHL's bow, serving notice that the young stars were ready for marquee billing.

A year later, the game's top stars reconvened in south Florida for the 2003 All-Star weekend. Among hockey's elite class for the first time were Young Guns graduates Heatley and Marian Gaborik, along with other All-Star Game freshmen such as Vincent Lecavalier, Olli Jokinen and Eric Brewer, as well as sophomores Marian Hossa and Joe Thornton.

"We're with the big dogs now," joked Heatley, as he held court at a beachfront hotel. Like lottery winners, some new members of this fraternity were awestruck by their status. "I wondered if I would get to wear my number in the game," Lecavalier said with a smile. "Then I bumped into Scott Stevens in the elevator and knew I wouldn't be wearing no. 4."

Gaborik, the soft-spoken Minnesota Wild forward, shuffled uncomfortably in his sandals as he wrestled with an unfamiliar language and burgeoning media demands.

"It has been a dream to be here, to play with players like Modano, Jagr and Naslund," he said. "I know I still have room for improvement."

Wide-eyed Eric Brewer, the Edmonton Oilers' defenceman, approached the weekend as if he were an apprentice studying at an advanced hockey seminar. "I'm inquisitive," said the young Canadian Olympian. "I like to study how players work, how they approach their business, how they get through a game."

Even for a returning All-Star such as Hossa, challenging for the Rocket Richard Trophy as the NHL's top goal scorer, the novelty of the weekend was still fresh. "It's a dream come true," the Senators star admitted. "My brother and I would stay up late at night in Slovakia to watch this game. It's a privilege to be here."

"PEOPLE LIKE TO SEE more versatile players. There are more of these players coming in, not one-dimensional players. They are the future and it looks bright with the talent we have here." — New Jersey Devils veteran Scott Stevens assessing the NHL stars of tomorrow

Respect among upper-echelon players is mutual. As these young players rubbed shoulders with perennial stars such as Patrick Roy, Paul Kariya and Al MacInnis, veterans acknowledged the rising tide of young role models in the league.

"If you're a kid, you want to be a Joe Thornton or Todd Bertuzzi," proclaimed St. Louis centre Doug Weight. "They're strong, and fast. They have it all. And most importantly, they believe in themselves."

"Heatley is a great talent," Scott Stevens assessed. "He's come a long way in a short time. I think people like to see more versatile players. There are more of these players coming in, not one-dimensional players. They are the future and it looks bright with the talent we have here."

That Saturday night, in cramped quarters, down the corridor from the All-Star dressing rooms, a new class of young stars nervously prepared for their opportunity under the bright lights.

Rick Nash, the NHL's first pick in the 2002 entry draft, looked ahead to the game with occasional glances toward the All-Star rooms. "Just to be a player in the NHL is an honour," said the Columbus forward, who had two goals in a Young Stars loss. "My goal one day is to be in the room down the hall."

Following the Young Stars contest, the "big dogs" took centre stage for the NHL super-skills events. A year removed from the freshman game, Marian Gaborik limbered up for the fastest-skater competition. Growing up, the young Slovak had idolized countryman Peter Bondra, a five-time All-Star participant and twice a winner of the NHL's fastest skater event.

"Gaborik has the fastest first two strides in the league," Minnesota teammate Cliff Ronning had informed me earlier in the season, prior to a *Hockey Night in Canada* telecast. "He's like a cross between Pavel Bure and Alexander Mogilny."

At the sound of the starter's whistle, Gaborik launched himself for one sizzling orbit around the Office Depot Center ice. When he stopped the clock 13.713 seconds later, Gaborik had verified Ronning's claims and topped the field by better than a half second. It was an astonishing, quicksilver performance, considering former winners Sergei Fedorov and Bill Guerin were in the field.

The following afternoon Dany Heatley boldly stroked his signature on the NHL's showcase game, just as fellow Thrasher Kovalchuk had at the Young Guns affair a year earlier. Heatley shredded legendary goaltender Patrick Roy twice in the first period, scoring his second goal by bunting a puck out of mid-air.

"I'd say the guy has a lot of talent to do that," an impressed Roy said following the game.

The 22-year-old Heatley counted two more in the second period against Jocelyn Thibault, matching an All-Star Game record shared by Mario Lemieux, Mike Gartner, Vincent Damphousse and Wayne Gretzky. The virtuoso performance inspired Gretzky to visit Heatley during the second intermission, urging the young star to break the record. "It was very meaningful," Heatley said of the visit. "I appreciated that."

In the third period, playing on a line with Olli Jokinen and boyhood hero Jaromir Jagr, Heatley was thwarted in his quest for the record. However, the Calgary product sprang Jokinen for a breakaway goal that sent the game to overtime and ultimately a shootout, during which Heatley also scored.

The young Thrasher was showered with praise and MVP honours. "He will be a superstar in this league for a long time," predicted veteran defenceman Al MacInnis.

Clearly, it was Heatley's day. And the most enduring message from that 2003 All-Star weekend was this: The NHL's "Generation Next" has arrived, and the future is bright. Dany Heatley, Marian Gaborik, Marian Hossa, Olli Jokinen, Rick Nash, Joe Thornton, Vincent Lecavalier, Eric Brewer, Ilya Kovalchuk and Mike Comrie: They are all part of that generation, which is already leaving its own unique stamp on the game. You can read each of their stories — as well as those of hockey's other young superstars — on the pages that follow.

— Chris Cuthbert
Hockey Night in Canada

ITECH
NTO

NIK ANTROPOV #80

TORONTO MAPLE LEAFS • CENTRE

Height: 6-5 Weight: 203 Born: February 18, 1980 – Vost, U.S.S.R.

Season	Team	GP	G	A	TP	PIM	+/-	Shots	Pct
1999–2000	Maple Leafs	66	12	18	30	41	14	89	13.48
2000–2001	Maple Leafs	52	6	11	17	30	5	71	8.45
2001–2002	Maple Leafs	11	1	1	2	4	-1	12	8.33
2002–2003	Maple Leafs	72	16	29	45	124	11	102	15.68
NHL Totals		201	35	59	94	199	29	274	12.77

Nothing strikes greater fear in the heart of a professional athlete than these three words: serious knee injury. Such misfortune can easily short-circuit a career — in hockey, football, baseball or basketball — not to mention all the dreams chased through years of sweat and dedication to a sport.

Nik Antropov has managed to overcome the dreaded affliction, not once but twice. At just 23 years old, the promising centreman with the Toronto Maple Leafs has already endured major surgical reconstructions on both knees. For a towering kid whose most glaring weakness as an up-and-coming NHL player was skating, those injuries could have quite easily proved career-ending.

They haven't, however. The Leafs have been patient with their project and, during the 2002–3 season, that patience began to pay some obvious dividends. Antropov emerged during his fourth NHL season, shaking off the nagging doubts caused by his injuries, to post easily his best campaign as an NHL forward. "The Kazakhstan Kid" scored 16 goals and added 29 assists to give Leafs fans a glimpse of what should be an outstanding future in the game.

"I think Antropov can be an All-Star player in this league," says teammate, sometime linemate and eight-year NHL veteran Mikael Renberg. "Nikki is definitely a guy who can score a lot of points."

"People questioned his skating," adds Leafs captain Mats Sundin, "but I think he's going to be a hell of a player."

Those kinds of forecasts would have been difficult to make regarding Antropov even a year earlier, when his third season with the Leafs was limited to just 11 games and he suffered his second major knee injury. He underwent surgery in February after hurting his knee while playing for Toronto's American Hockey League farm team, the St. John's, Newfoundland, Maple Leafs, and faced his second lengthy recovery period in just three years.

"I can't even tell you," Antropov says now, when asked just how low the injuries had him feeling. "It was pretty tough for me. I can't even say. You have to fight through it anyway, just be mentally ready and you'll be all right."

The mental aspect of recovery has been more difficult than the physical rehabilitation, says the young centre. Hockey players tend to be susceptible to knee injuries, but the knees can take an extra pounding when your frame is as big as that of Antropov, who is six foot five and 203 pounds.

"First of all, probably the mental part of my game is improving," he says now. "I struggled the first couple of years with my knee surgeries and my mental part because of that. Both my physical part of my play and my mental game are better and that's the

"IT'S TIME AND EXPERIENCE. It's not something you can rush. It's a lot like Todd Bertuzzi's situation in Vancouver."
—Leafs assistant general manager Mike Penny on Antropov's development

biggest part. Two ACLs [the anterior cruciate ligament, in the knee] are the two most major injuries you can get in the NHL and all sports and I got them in three years, so it's pretty tough."

Nikolai Antropov was born on February 18, 1980, in the former Soviet Union city of Vost. He was raised in Ust-Kamenogorsk, an industrial centre of about 325,000 people in east Kazakhstan. The city, which sits on the junction of the Irtysh and Ulba rivers, was founded in 1720 as a Russian military outpost in the foothills of the Rudnyy Altai mountains. It has evolved into the centre of Kazakhstan's hockey culture, with the hometown Torpedoes competing against the top professional teams of Russia and producing eight NHL draftees, including San Jose Sharks goalie Evgeni Nabokov, the 2001 NHL rookie of the year.

Antropov began skating at age four and playing hockey not long after. His boyhood idol was Mario Lemieux and by the time he was 16 the gangly prospect was already playing for the Torpedoes in the Russian professional league's second division, going up against men many years older and more experienced.

He drew the attention of North American scouts during his second Russian League season with Ust-Kamenogorsk, when he scored 15 goals and added 24 assists in 42 games for the Torpedoes. Scouts liked his size and the fact that he clearly had a physical, aggressive edge to his game, racking up 62 penalty minutes that season. He also impressed talent evaluators while representing Kazakhstan at the world junior championships in Helsinki.

The Leafs took what some thought to be a gamble on the lanky Kazakh at the 1998 NHL entry draft in Buffalo when they accepted the advice of then Toronto scout Anders Hedberg and used the 10th overall pick to select Antropov. Although other teams certainly had Antropov on their radar screens, Toronto surprised pundits by picking the prospect that high.

Antropov didn't join Toronto's organization right away, instead moving up to Dynamo Moscow of the Russian Superligue, where he posted 14 points in 30 games as an 18-year-old. When he did join the Leafs a season later, the 19-year-old faced the expected language and cultural difficulties, although Toronto had several Russian players in its system and that helped Antropov adjust. Over his four NHL seasons, he has subsequently developed a command of the language although it is still spoken with a thick accent.

"I've been here long enough," Antropov says now. "It wasn't a big deal. First couple of years we had, like, seven Russians on the team, so that helped me and now I feel pretty confident and comfortable."

Antropov broke into the NHL in impressive fashion during the 1999–2000 season, putting up 30 points, including 12 goals, in 66 games and finishing a noteworthy plus-14 for the year. His first NHL point came in his very first game, against the Florida Panthers. And just over two months later he turned in the highlight of his rookie season when he scored three times against the same Panthers, marking the first time in 10 years that a Leafs rookie had managed a hat trick.

As much as his point production, the Leafs liked the fact that their newest addition showed no fear of the rough going in the NHL, contributing 79 hits to go along with his obvious offensive input that rookie season. "He's just a kid. He still has to grow muscles," teammate and Leafs resident tough guy Tie Domi told the *Toronto Sun* at the time. "But he has shown that he isn't afraid of anyone out there."

But Antropov injured his right knee during his first appearance in the NHL playoffs and the great things expected of him in Year 2 never materialized. The surgery required and a subsequent infection which set in limited him to just 52 games in that second season, which he finished with six goals, 11 assists and 53 hits. In his third North American campaign, he played just 11 games and scored only two points for the big club.

While playing for the St. John's Maple Leafs in February 2002, Antropov's career outlook declined even further when he injured his left knee. The news was bad: That knee would also require surgery and extensive rehabilitation.

Antropov's long-term future with the Leafs seemed a little uncertain. His name continually popped up in trade rumours surrounding the club, first in speculated deals as Toronto attempted to secure Eric Lindros and later in possible attempts to acquire Alexei Kovalev.

Although the injuries caused many to doubt whether he would ever reach the levels the Leafs envisioned when they drafted him, Antropov made some serious strides in that direction during his breakthrough 2002–3 season. Playing most of the year, he posted

career-high marks of 16 goals, 29 assists, 45 points and 124 penalty minutes. Perhaps most importantly, he dressed for 72 regular-season games.

Antropov didn't stay as healthy for the playoffs, however. A foot injury allowed him to dress for only three games of the Leafs' disappointing seven-game setback against the Philadelphia Flyers in the first round. After injuring the foot in Game 1, Antropov managed to return for Games 6 and 7 but went pointless in the playoffs, just one more bit of bad news for Leafs fans who watched their team humbled 6-1 by the physical Flyers in Game 7.

Most Leafs' fans are hoping Antropov can play a huge role for the team as it tries to rebound from the first-round loss to the Flyers and the unexpected early exit from the playoffs in 2003.

Leafs assistant general manager and director of player personnel Mike Penny says Antropov "has overcome the confidence [troubles] that come with having had two serious knee operations." Penny says a big factor in Antropov's development has been Toronto head coach and general manager Pat Quinn and the time he has allowed the young forward to mature.

"Pat Quinn has been very patient with him," Penny says. "It's time and experience.

It's not something you can rush. It's a lot like Todd Bertuzzi's situation in Vancouver."

The comparison with Bertuzzi may seem a tad generous to Antropov, but the Vancouver Canucks' big winger took his time to develop at the NHL level, too. Bertuzzi, who at six foot three is similar in size to Antropov, missed most of his fourth season due to a leg injury and didn't manage to crack the 40-point plateau until his sixth season in the NHL.

While Antropov's skating is still the second thing that's questioned after the condition of his knees, his skills with the puck, great vision on the ice, tremendous size and reach and willingness to mix it up are enough to overcome his only clear deficiency as a player.

During much of his breakout season, he was able to skate with two of the Leafs' more talented veteran players — captain Mats Sundin and fellow Russian Alex Mogilny — and later in the season with newcomer Owen Nolan.

"It is important because they are older guys and they've got lots of experience in the NHL, especially in the playoffs," Antropov says of the value of playing with seasoned linemates. "So you have to take what you can from playing with them. It's been a great advantage to play with Alex and Mats — it's helped a lot."

Most importantly, says teammate Mikael Renberg, is that Antropov is simply playing more. Confidence at the NHL level often comes as a direct result of ice time. The more a player is out there, the more comfortable he usually becomes.

"First of all, he plays a lot more than he did before and he gets more confidence by getting more ice time," Renberg says, when asked what the biggest difference was for Antropov in 2002–3. "You can tell by him having the puck. Sometimes it looks like it's impossible to knock the puck off of him, he's so strong all over the ice."

That strength and size help to make Antropov a special physical talent. But, like Bertuzzi, he also possesses big-league skill. The package, if it can hang together without breaking down, is a dangerous one.

"He sees the ice really well and he knows where all his teammates are on the ice, it seems like," Renberg says. "He's big and strong and very, very good with the puck. He's probably getting a little better as a skater, but he's also developed the other skills, so it's a combination. He uses his other skills so well that it turns him into a great player."

Former Leafs scout Anders Hedberg, upon whose recommendation the Leafs chose Antropov in the 1998 draft, feels the best is yet to come.

"You haven't seen anything from this kid, yet," Hedberg told the *National Post.* "He's just starting to regain his confidence from the two surgeries. There is no limit as to how good he can be." HYS

THE NUMBERS GAME

Nik Antropov graciously agreed to give up his familiar no. 11 sweater when the Toronto Maple Leafs acquired Owen Nolan in a late-season 2003 trade with the San Jose Sharks. The minor hockey association in Nolan's hometown of Thorold, Ontario, retired no. 11 in his honour a few years ago and he was happy to be able to keep the same no. he wore with the Sharks. Antropov now wears no. 80, signifying the year in which he was born.

TPS
NEW YORK
RANGERS
RANGER
TPS
TPS

DAN BLACKBURN #31

NEW YORK RANGERS • GOALIE

Height: 6-0 Weight: 180 Born: May 20, 1983 – Montreal

Season	Team	GMS	MIN	W	L	T	GA	SO	Avg
2001–2002	Rangers	31	1737	12	16	0	95	0	3.28
2002–2003	Rangers	32	1762	8	16	4	93	1	3.17
NHL Totals		63	3499	20	32	4	188	1	3.23

Every so often the videotapes would arrive in the mail in Baden, Germany, and young Dan Blackburn would be waiting for them. They were sent from Montreal by his aunt and uncle and they included television programs from Canada. Most importantly, they included hockey and, of course, the Montreal Canadiens.

"Dan went over and over and over those tapes," recalls Blackburn's mother, Hope Clark. "I didn't think at the time that he actually knew what he was watching. But he would rewind them and he would watch them for hours. It was like he was studying something. I had no idea the intense focus he was putting into it."

Not surprising then, that when the Blackburn family returned to Montreal in the summer of 1989, six-year-old Dan wanted to try the exciting sport that he had seen on those videotapes. So his mother signed him up for a week-long summer hockey school.

He hadn't skated much before that, so Dan began that week with his hands clenching the edge of the boards, pulling himself around the rink while the other players whizzed by.

"By the end of the second day, he could skate," his mother says. "But he was still by far the poorest skater on the ice. So he decided he would put himself in goal, because then he wouldn't have to skate so much."

Since then, Dan Blackburn has never left the crease. And he has never stopped improving as a goaltender, going in just a dozen years from that shaky start at a Montreal hockey school into the crease of the New York Rangers. He is one of the youngest goaltenders ever to play in the NHL, joining the Rangers as an 18-year-old during the 2001–2 season.

Blackburn spent part of his childhood — between the ages of three and six — in the Black Forest area of Germany. His father, a schoolteacher, had been hired to teach the children of Canadian Armed Forces members overseas. His mother, meanwhile, worked as a drug and alcohol counsellor, as well as teaching English as a second language to French-Canadian soldiers.

Dan was just two when he began going to German kinderschool. By his second year, he was fluent in German. "He's a very quick study," Hope says.

That attribute also translated to hockey, even before Dan actually hit the ice. Those videotapes that had arrived in the mail from Canada also included the crease heroics of the Canadiens' brilliant young "butterfly" netminder of the time, Patrick Roy. And Roy's glorious talent and penchant for the dramatic save became a particular focus for the transplanted Canadian kid growing up more than an ocean away.

Despite his wobbly beginnings on the ice, Dan quickly became a standout minor-hockey goaltender after his return to Canada. The family lived in Montreal until 1992, when his mother and father split up. Dan moved to Toronto with his mother and, a year later, the pair relocated to Canmore, Alberta, a small community near the ski resort of Banff in the Rocky Mountains.

Hope worked seven days a week after the move to Canmore, but her son kept busy playing hockey. The pair was helped out by other parents in Canmore who drove Dan to games and practices when Hope couldn't. "The people of Canmore have just been such a key part in Dan's hockey development," she says.

As a youngster Blackburn was always big for his age, and athletic. He was a good soccer and baseball player, but he truly loved being on the ice playing goal. It was a position in which he never had to take a shift off and was always a key part of any game.

By the time he was in grade 9, Blackburn was already playing with the Bow Valley Eagles of the Alberta Junior Hockey League. As a 14-year-old he played in 20 games with the tier 2 club, going 9-6-1 with one shutout and a 3.35 goals-against average. The next year, at just 15, he played in 38 games, going 7-19 with a 4.51 average.

The Eagles were not a great team for either of Blackburn's two seasons, but playing there allowed him to remain at home in Canmore while still getting two years of junior experience and facing plenty of shots.

Those two years were enough to get Dan ready for his next step to the Western Hockey League. The Edmonton Ice had chosen Blackburn third overall in the WHL's bantam draft of 14-year-old players, making him the highest goaltender ever selected. But during his time in Bow Valley, the Ice had relocated to Cranbrook, British Columbia, and become known as the Kootenay Ice.

"There had been a camp in Lethbridge before that bantam draft and our scouts came back raving about Blackburn," recalls Jeff Chynoweth, now the general manager and vice-president of the Ice after being with the junior franchise since its inception. "Dan was a great pick for us, because great goaltending is the most important position, at any level of hockey."

The step meant Blackburn had to leave home, something his mother knew had been coming as her son progressed through minor hockey. But that didn't make the move any easier. "That was really the official move away from home," Hope says. "We had gone through a long mental process deciding whether he should go to college or the WHL. In the process, I had sort of got used to the idea of the WHL. But it was still hard because he'd always been with me."

Dan Blackburn made a seamless transition from the AJHL to the much faster, more physical WHL, however. Despite the fact that he was just 16, the Ice decided to rotate starts between Blackburn and returning veteran B. J. Boxma to begin the season. That arrangement lasted only a month. "From November on, Danny asserted himself as our no. 1 guy," Chynoweth recalls.

Blackburn went on to play 51 games that rookie WHL season, posting an impressive 34-8-7 record and a goals-against average of 2.52. During the playoffs he led the Ice to their first WHL championship, becoming the youngest player to ever capture WHL playoff MVP honours, and helped his team into the Memorial Cup national tournament in Halifax. He went 16-5 with a 2.03 average and was named rookie of the year in the WHL and all of Canadian major junior hockey. He also posted an impressive .912 save percentage.

The next year, despite a groin injury that slowed him early in the season, his numbers were once again excellent: 33-14-2 with a 2.77 average. That was enough to earn him Canadian major junior goalie-of-the-year and all-star honours.

Better still, his two years in the WHL prompted the New York Rangers to select Blackburn with their first pick, 10th overall, in the 2001 NHL entry draft, making him the highest goalie selected in franchise history.

Both his parents and grandparents came to the draft. And so did Gerri and Mort Geller of Montreal, the aunt and uncle who had sent those Canadiens' hockey tapes to him in Germany. Nobody knew where Dan would go in the draft and the family even held a lottery, during which they each took their best guess. "Dan wrote down that he was going to be drafted by New York and the Rangers had never even talked to him at that point," Hope says.

STUDENT OF THE GAME

As the son of two schoolteachers, the value of education was instilled early in Dan Blackburn. He was an honour-roll student and was named Alberta Junior Hockey League scholastic player of the year during each of his two seasons in the tier 2 league. "Education has always been a high priority for us," says Blackburn's mother, Hope Clark.

Most observers expected him to be back in Cranbrook for at least another season of junior hockey. But Dan Blackburn went to the Rangers' training camp as an 18-year-old and never returned. The turn of events surprised his mother, who had moved to Kimberley over the summer partly because she thought her son would play another year in nearby Cranbrook. It also surprised the Ice, who expected Dan to return.

For most players, going to the NHL, particularly New York, at 18 wouldn't be a good situation. The pressure and media scrutiny on professional athletes in that city is more intense than anywhere else in North America. But Chynoweth says Blackburn is a special individual. "Nothing Danny does surprises me," he says. "He's that good."

Blackburn appeared in 31 games with the struggling Rangers as a rookie, finishing with

"HE'S SO MATURE for his age, visualizes things and prepares well. Nothing rattles Danny." —Kootenay Ice vice-president and general manager Jeff Chynoweth

a 12-16-0 record and a 3.28 average on a poor defensive team. Near the end of the season he posted a five-game winning streak and he made the NHL All-Rookie Team for his efforts. His NHL debut came on October 10 against the Washington Capitals, making him the fifth-youngest goalie to ever play in the league, at 18 years and 143 days.

Blackburn joined a Rangers franchise that, for the most part in recent seasons, has dramatically under-achieved considering its talent level. His teammates suddenly included stars such as Mark Messier, Eric Lindros, Pavel Bure and Brian Leetch and he was playing behind Mike Richter, one of the best goalies in the NHL.

Adding to the intimidation potential was the fact that, shortly after joining the Rangers, Blackburn found himself in downtown Manhattan on the day terrorists attacked the World Trade Center. "Dan phoned me within 15 minutes of it happening," says Hope. "He said: 'Mom, I'm fine.' I was a little concerned then because he was totally alone there."

Shortly afterward, however, former Rangers goaltender and current broadcaster John Davidson invited Blackburn to live with his family at his home in Westchester, an upscale suburban area north of the Bronx. A year living with Davidson, who helped show the youngster the ropes and also travelled with the Rangers, eased Blackburn's transition.

Early in his second season with the Rangers, Dan Blackburn moved into his own place in Trump Towers, a high-rise overlooking the Hudson River and just a couple of blocks from Central Park. "He's a New Yorker now," says his mother. "He really likes the city. He likes the restaurants. He likes the life."

Playing in the NHL so early has put some pressure on him, however. When veteran Mike Richter was sidelined with post-concussion syndrome early in the 2002–3 season, Blackburn started 18 straight games, going 7-8-2. "Here's a 19-year-old kid, a New York team riding on him, and I don't think there is a player on the team, a coach, or anyone in management worried," John Davidson told the *New York Post* in November. "Nobody worries about Dan."

Still, general manager Glen Sather obviously wasn't comfortable with the Rangers' hopes riding on the shoulders of a teenager. Trying to avoid an embarrassing sixth straight season out of the playoffs despite a payroll that topped $70 million US, the Rangers acquired 30-year-old veteran Mike Dunham from the Nashville Predators on December 12. After that, Dan Blackburn was relegated to a backup role. And there are some who wonder if Dunham's presence puts a question mark on Blackburn's status as the goalie of the future in the Big Apple.

With Blackburn, however, the key word is still "future." Heading into his third season with the Rangers he had yet to reach his 21st birthday. Most goaltending prospects haven't even pulled on an NHL uniform at that age. In the 2002–3 season Blackburn finished with a 3.17 goals-against average, down slightly from his rookie season. He appeared in 32 games, posting an 8-16-4 record and a save percentage of .890.

The highlight of the season for Blackburn came on November 7, when he made 26 saves at Madison Square Garden to beat the Calgary Flames 1-0 and earn his first NHL shutout, with his mother in the stands.

Another ray of light near the end of the season came when Blackburn backstopped the Rangers to a 2-1 win over the Philadelphia Flyers to temporarily keep New York's playoff hopes alive. The sophomore goalie made 28 saves in two periods after relieving the injured Dunham.

Those who know him expect Dan Blackburn to make the most of this learning experience. He has always been a serious student, learning, absorbing and waiting for his chance to put what he's learned into practice.

"He's so mature for his age, visualizes things and prepares well," says Jeff Chynoweth. "Nothing rattles Danny. His focus and preparation is better than any athlete I've ever been associated with. In my 17 years in this league, he's the best goaltender I've ever been associated with.

"He can be a star in the NHL in the right circumstances." HYS

CINTAS
UNIFORM PEOPLE
EASTON

JAY BOUWMEESTER #4

FLORIDA PANTHERS • DEFENCE

Height: 6-4 Weight: 210 Born: September 27, 1983 – Edmonton

Season	Team	GP	G	A	TP	PIM	+/-	Shots	Pct
2002–2003	Panthers	82	4	12	16	14	-29	110	3.63
NHL Totals		82	4	12	16	14	-29	110	3.63

He wasn't born with skates on. It only seems that way when Jay Bouwmeester gobbles up the glistening surface with huge, effortless strides as he prowls the ice for the young Florida Panthers.

But it wasn't all that long after Gena Bouwmeester gave birth to her strapping baby boy in Edmonton on September 27, 1983, that young Jay was indeed skating. He had barely taken his first steps when mom came downstairs one day to discover the toddler had somehow managed to lace on his older sister's white, four-wheel roller skates and was taking a solo spin around the basement.

So, if it appears Bouwmeester has been skating forever as the fresh-faced teen makes an immediate impact in hockey's big leagues, well, he practically has.

"I remember the first time I got him skating," recalls Dan Bouwmeester, who had his son on real ice skates on a backyard rink in the south Edmonton suburb of Mill Woods before Jay had reached his second birthday. "I was holding him up to make sure he was okay and he just started shouting: 'Let me go! Let me go!' He just kind of took off, walking around on his skates, and then he really got going. It was very natural for him."

"Natural" is an appropriate word to describe Jay Bouwmeester, a six-foot-four, 210-pounder who became a solid contributor on the Panthers' blue line as an 18-year-old rookie. That's a rare accomplishment in the NHL for a teen playing defence — a position that usually takes years for a young puck professional to master.

But Dan Bouwmeester doesn't seem surprised that his son has been able to make the step up in such smooth fashion, instantly becoming a top 4 defenceman on coach Mike Keenan's young Panther team and receiving regular power-play and penalty-killing time despite his considerable lack of experience. For that matter, Jay himself isn't surprised, either.

In interviews, when his voice barely registers over the dressing room din on the tape recorders of reporters, and even with some teammates, the lanky, blue-eyed Bouwmeester comes across as shy. But underneath is actually a quiet calm that comes from a rock-solid confidence in his own abilities. You won't hear this fair-haired kid blowing his own horn, but neither will you see him backing down from a challenge.

"I mean, that was the goal this year, to make the team," Bouwmeester said simply during his rookie year, when asked if he had surprised himself with his early strides as a Panther. "It was something I was looking forward to. It's a big step up. But as you go through the exhibitions, you get to feel a little more comfortable and, I guess, you get used to your surroundings."

Bouwmeester has certainly appeared at ease since he was chosen No. 3 overall in the NHL entry draft by the Panthers in June 2002. Right from the start, Florida head coach Mike Keenan told reporters that Bouwmeester would probably be able to contribute immediately. By midseason the youngster was already averaging more than 17 minutes a game and seeing action in every situation.

"BOUWMEESTER has a unique combination of hockey sense, skating ability and stick skills ... I've never seen an 18-year-old who's got the complete package like him."
— Former Florida Panthers assistant coach Paul Baxter

That playing time — the confidence the demanding Keenan has shown in Bouwmeester — was the true measuring stick. Bouwmeester's rookie performance couldn't be measured in points, as it could with a centre or a winger. But if he had been a liability on the ice, he wouldn't have played. "Jay's come into a situation as a young player and was given an opportunity," Keenan says. "I think he's really developed his game well. He's playing a lot of minutes for a 19-year-old on defence in the NHL."

But before he could play defence, before he could play real hockey, Jay Bouwmeester first had to be able to skate. Dan Bouwmeester didn't want his son playing organized games until he could really wheel, so Jay didn't join a team until he was six. He took to the ice with Dan, a former University of Alberta Golden Bear defenceman, in the backyard and between periods of Golden Bear alumni games.

When Jay did start playing organized hockey, he was immediately a top player. He was a natural at just about every sport he tried, including baseball and volleyball, but hockey was his main focus. He was always big for his age but, unlike other tall teens, he never seemed to suffer through any awkward, uncoordinated stage.

Jay's development was aided by the support of his parents, both schoolteachers in Edmonton. Dan also served as Jay's coach in Mill Woods until, as a bantam, the youngster joined Edmonton's Southside Athletic Club, which has a rule against fathers coaching their sons. "Both my parents were very supportive growing up and that's something I'm really thankful for," Jay says.

Unlike many other parents of minor-hockey prodigies, however, Dan Bouwmeester didn't want his son playing above his age group. Fortunately, there was plenty of talent in the Edmonton area at the time and Jay developed quickly playing with and against his own peer group. In 1997–98, Bouwmeester helped lead the Southside Athletic Club to the Alberta bantam AAA championship.

"You're talking to a dad, and I think every dad thinks his son is going to be the next Wayne Gretzky or Bobby Orr," says Dan Bouwmeester. "I knew he was special, but as a teacher and a coach I see kids who are special all the time who don't pan out or who lose their interest for some reason. Still, I was quietly confident."

Others were confident, too. Player agents began phoning the family home in Edmonton when Jay was barely 14 and he became the No. 1 selection in the Western Hockey League's 1998 bantam draft by the Medicine Hat Tigers. His father had taken him to Edmonton Ice games as a young teen and Jay had made playing in the WHL an early goal. There wasn't much thought about the U.S. college route. He was ready for the longer schedule of the WHL and the chance to prove himself in the more rugged major junior style of play. "A kid with his size and talent — the WHL was the way to go," Dan says now.

What that meant for the Bouwmeesters, however, was saying goodbye to their son at a tender age. Jay was still only 15 and in his final season of bantam when he joined the Tigers for a few games. But the next season, as a 16-year-old, he moved to Medicine Hat, Alberta — nearly five hours southwest of Edmonton by car — full-time. Dan Bouwmeester will never forget that first training camp and leaving his son in Medicine Hat. On the lonely drive home, "I remember thinking: 'What are we doing here? Are we doing the right thing?'"

Medicine Hat Tigers general manager Rick Carriere was certain he was doing the right thing by taking Bouwmeester No. 1 among all the bantam players in Alberta. He had first seen Jay as a peewee and, like so many others, had immediately tagged him as a future NHLer because of the youngster's combination of size, skating ability, puck-handling and unflappable demeanour.

What Carriere and others saw in Bouwmeester was skating ability that was astounding for such a big body. The kid was able to get up in the rush with the forwards and still be the first one back on defence. Perhaps former Tigers coach Bob Loucks put it best when he told *The Hockey News*, "He skates better than most people walk."

Bouwmeester worked hard to develop all his skills during three seasons in "The Hat," a southern Alberta junior hockey hotbed that has produced its share of NHLers including Lanny McDonald and Trevor Linden. The Tigers struggled during his stay there — they had 13 rookies in Bouwmeester's first junior season — and they never did make the playoffs. But Bouwmeester proved the consummate team guy while honing his skills, spending hours in the weight room and staying after practice to get himself ready for the next level.

His numbers improved as he settled in, going from the 34 points he compiled as a junior rookie to nearly double that — at 11 goals and 50 assists — in the 2001–2 WHL season. NHL scouts drooled over his skating ability and puck skills, realizing that his individual

NOW THAT'S QUIET

Jay Bouwmeester's game did most of the talking for him during his rookie season with the Florida Panthers. In fact, the topic of just how quiet the teenager is became something of a running joke. "When you're with Jay, it's like you've got your own room on the road," teammate Lance Ward quipped to reporters in December. "I look over and I'm not sure he's breathing. He doesn't snore, he sits so still. The kid is so quiet he tiptoes to the bathroom at night."

numbers probably would have been far higher had his team been a contender, where his defensive responsibilities wouldn't have been so demanding and he would have had more finishers up front.

While he never made the playoffs with the Tigers, Bouwmeester did excel internationally as a junior. At 16 years and three months, he was the youngest-ever player selected for Canada's world junior team in 2000, winning a bronze medal and outstanding-player honours in the semifinal game against Russia. Bouwmeester and Jason Spezza of the Mississauga Ice Dogs were both selected as 16-year-olds, joining only Wayne Gretzky and Eric Lindros as players who have had the honour of pulling on the maple-leaf jersey that young. He also played in two subsequent world junior tournaments, winning a silver in 2002.

Throughout Bouwmeester's draft year, he was the No. 1-rated prospect by NHL Central Scouting and projected to be top pick by almost everybody for the June 22 selection at Toronto's Air Canada Centre. But that isn't how it worked out. The Panthers held first pick and were prepared to take Bouwmeester with it, but they were able to swing a deal with the Columbus Blue Jackets to swap first-round selections, still guarantee themselves the right to draft Bouwmeester at No. 3 by making a side deal with Atlanta, and likely improve their draft status for 2003 — all because Columbus, which initially held the No. 3 position, wanted to ensure it would land London Knights left-winger Rick Nash.

As a result, draft day went a little differently than the Bouwmeesters had envisioned. Instead of being selected No. 1, the crowning achievement to a sterling minor-hockey career, Jay had been forced to suffer through some early draft-table confusion and then settle for going third overall. Publicly, at least, he didn't seem to mind the way it had evolved. Playing in the NHL and getting a chance to contribute right away for the Panthers was enough.

Still, in retrospect Dan Bouwmeester feels his son was the unfortunate victim of the cutthroat business side of pro hockey. "I think it will bother Jay later in life," Dan says. "I think he got robbed of a very deserving honour, a once-in-a-lifetime honour, and I'm not happy with that."

Any sting the draft-day dealings might have caused faded quickly, however, as it became clear that the Panthers had reserved a big space in their future for Bouwmeester. He settled into a posh south Florida apartment complex in which several of his teammates lived and allowed himself the luxury of a new truck.

On the ice, Bouwmeester has already turned plenty of heads with his fluid skating, positional play, puck-handling and crisp passing. "Bouwmeester has a unique combination of hockey sense, skating ability and stick skills," says Paul Baxter, an assistant coach with the Panthers during Bouwmeester's rookie year. "You know, this is my 29th year in professional hockey and I've never seen an 18-year-old who's got the complete package like him. He seems to be at the 26- or 27-year-old level and I'm not talking about average players, I'm talking top players. He's been like that since training camp."

Making the jump from small-town Medicine Hat, population 51,000, to a large, glamorous city such as Miami has been a big change for Bouwmeester. While south Florida is a world apart from southern Alberta, Bouwmeester admits that not having his play held under a microscope there, as it might be in a hockey hotbed such as Toronto, is probably a positive thing for a rookie. The talented Panthers lineup, dotted with youngsters such as Olli Jokinen, Stephen Weiss and goaltender Roberto Luongo, has also provided an interesting incubator for Bouwmeester, who is certainly not alone in adjusting to the NHL on the fly. "On a veteran team, he might be brought along a bit differently," Keenan admits. "But he's in his element with a bunch of young guys here who are learning to play together."

While those who best know Bouwmeester rave about his down-to-earth personality, it is ironically his personality that has spawned the only criticism of the Panthers' top pick. In the opinion of some, he is too quiet.

Baxter said some scouts from other NHL teams questioned Bouwmeester going No. 1 in the draft because he hadn't shown a mean streak during his WHL career, not fighting once during his three years with the Tigers. Others wondered if he had the toughness to be a true defensive star in the NHL. Baxter, who piled up 1,564 penalty minutes during eight rugged NHL seasons, laughs off the thought that Bouwmeester is somehow lacking in that department, saying, "He competes very hard." Carriere, the Medicine Hat Tigers' general manager, says if people are reading weakness into Jay's quiet nature, they're wrong. "I think anybody who makes those criticisms of him would love to have him as a son," Carriere says. "He's a team guy all the way."

A quiet nature isn't necessarily a negative, argues Jay's father. "I think it's a media thing," Dan Bouwmeester says, "I see those [stories] and it really upsets me. It's like he's got to be a pro athlete and a movie star. All the kid wants to do is be the best athlete he can be."

Nitpicking aside, virtually everybody agrees Jay Bouwmeester has a terrific future as an NHL blueliner and he is already drawing comparisons with Chris Pronger and Wade Redden. Perhaps tellingly, as a youngster Jay admired the Detroit Red Wings' classy captain Steve Yzerman, a quiet, lead-by-example NHL superstar. "Everybody is their own person, their own player," Bouwmeester says.

Bouwmeester's NHL beginnings were good enough that *Hockey Night in Canada*'s Don Cherry was already touting him in December as the "hands-down" leading candidate for rookie of the year. That proved to be premature, however, as Bouwmeester finished with an unimpressive minus-29 rating playing for a Panther team that faded from the playoff picture. Nevertheless, he logged nearly 20 minutes a game and finished his first NHL season with four goals and 12 assists. That was good enough to earn him an invitation to join Team Canada at the 2003 world championships in Helsinki, where he tallied seven points and was named the tournament's top defenceman while leading Canada to the Gold.

"He's just starting to figure it all out [at the NHL level]," Baxter says. "You know, there are already times in games where he says 'I'm taking over,' and he does just that." HYS

CCM
EASTON
EASTON
TE
upport Canada

ERIC BREWER #2

EDMONTON OILERS • DEFENCE

Height: 6-3 Weight: 220 Born: April 17, 1979 — Vernon, BC

Season	Team	GP	G	A	TP	PIM	+/-	Shots	Pct
1998–1999	Islanders	63	5	6	11	32	-14	63	7.93
1999–2000	Islanders	26	0	2	2	20	-11	30	0.0
2000–2001	Oilers	77	7	14	21	53	15	91	7.69
2001–2002	Oilers	81	7	18	25	45	-5	165	4.24
2002–2003	Oilers	80	8	21	29	45	-11	147	5.44
NHL Totals		327	27	61	88	195	-26	496	5.44

At first, he couldn't really see himself playing on defence. Six-year-old Eric Brewer wanted to be up with the forwards during minor-hockey games in Ashcroft, British Columbia. Like most Canadian kids who could hold a hockey stick, he wanted to be wherever there was a chance to score some goals.

Fast forward 18 years, however, and it's difficult to imagine Eric Brewer playing anywhere other than the blue-line position he patrols with authority for the Edmonton Oilers of the NHL.

"The first couple of years you're playing minor hockey, everybody's really just moving around in a big crowd," Brewer recalls with a chuckle. "I think it was in atom [at age nine] that I actually became a defenceman. I wasn't crazy about it at first, but I was one of the strongest kids at skating backwards ..."

And that, basically, was it. Eric's dad Frank, a former defenceman himself who had managed to reach the junior ranks, encouraged his only son to play defence. Since Frank Brewer was also his son's minor-hockey coach until the time Eric was 14, that encouragement carried a little extra weight.

"That's kind of how he ended up playing defence," says the elder Brewer, a telecommunications employee in Kamloops.

Frank remembers Eric as a "quiet, average kid who never seemed to get into any trouble." He and his wife, Anna, herself an avid athlete in track and field, softball and curling, were always keeping Eric and his younger sister, Kristi, active.

"Eric was always busy. He played softball and he played tons of street hockey," Frank recalls. "Street hockey kept him always around home, on the driveway — he and all the neighbourhood kids."

Despite Eric having good size and some natural ability at most sports he tried, including softball and tennis, Frank said he didn't think seriously about his son playing professional hockey during those early years.

"I guess everybody does dream about it in the back of their minds, but the reality is a whole bunch of kids don't make it," he says. "There are so many good hockey players out there and there are so many variables involved."

Eric Brewer might have seemed average to his dad, but junior-hockey scouts thought differently. The youngster's well-honed skating skills — his first strides came at the age of three — size and ability to hit were enough to make him a top junior prospect by the time he became a teenager.

The Brewers struggled to decide whether Eric should opt for the major junior Western Hockey League or try to land a U.S. college scholarship by playing tier 2 junior hockey. But after a successful tryout with the Prince George Cougars, the family decided being on a nearby WHL team would be a good situation for him. And playing in the league was appealing since he had grown up watching the hometown Kamloops Blazers of the WHL.

"The Cougars told us he would probably be playing regularly by Christmas of his first year," Frank says. "We decided that would be a good situation because Prince George is only six hours away [by car] and he would be playing games in Kelowna and Kamloops and we would be able to see him there, too. But it is a tough thing to talk about your 16-year-old leaving home. You don't want to see him go away."

Easing the transition was the hospitable home of Vic and Suzann Aubichon, who billeted Brewer during his three years in Prince George. "I loved it there," Brewer says of the move. "It was tough for the first little bit to get used to a new city, but within a few weeks I was set."

The move proved a good one for Brewer, who consistently improved during his three years and eventually became a fan favourite in the B.C. Interior city. But he wasn't immediately an impact player in the WHL.

"He was a big, raw-boned kid, who was a good skater," recalls Ed Dempsey, who was head coach with the rival Kamloops Blazers when Brewer first broke into the WHL and later also coached the defenceman in Prince George. "Eric had a lot of potential and a huge upside for a 16-year-old, but he wasn't a dominant force right away."

Brewer blossomed slowly but steadily in the heat of the major junior game. He posted four goals and 10 assists as a rookie in the 1994–95 season and nearly doubled that total (5-24) during his second year with the Cougars. At the end of that sophomore season, Prince George went on a surprising run through the playoffs, reaching the Western Conference final. Dempsey, who was still coaching in Kamloops then, remembers that playoff run as the time Eric Brewer truly began to shine as an NHL prospect.

That performance, along with his six-foot-three, 220-pound frame and obvious skating ability, was enough to prompt the New York Islanders to select him fifth overall during the 1997 entry draft in Pittsburgh. Frank and Anna Brewer made the trip to the Pennsylvania steel town to see their son selected.

"It was pretty awesome, really,"' Frank recalls. "We didn't really have any preference where he went. I was just hoping for any team which would give him a shot at playing regularly."

"Honestly, I was just really excited to play in the NHL," Eric says. "It's great playing in Canada now, but when you're drafted by New York, that's where you go."

First, however, Brewer returned to Prince George to play another season of junior as an 18-year-old. Ed Dempsey took over the head coaching job with the Cougars that same fall but, unfortunately for him and his new team, Eric Brewer suffered a deep thigh bruise and was able to play less than half a season.

Nevertheless, in the 34 games he did dress, Brewer managed to improve his numbers from the previous season, finishing with five goals and 33 points. He also skated for Team Canada as it finished eighth in the world junior tournament at Helsinki.

"He really blossomed during his time in Prince George," Dempsey says now. "He just developed so well physically. Everything developed. His skating improved. His shot became a big-league shot. His on-ice awareness improved. He really learned how to read the game. He hadn't really been a confident guy his first couple of years in Prince George. But once he got that confidence, he just took off."

Dempsey, who remembers Eric as "an excellent kid, a very good student and a low-maintenance guy both on and off the ice," hoped to have Brewer back in Prince George as a 19-year-old but the New York Islanders decided to keep him in the NHL. The veteran junior coach thought that was a mistake on the part of the Islanders and, in hindsight, he was probably right.

"He would have been better off to come back and be a dominant 19-year-old in junior," Dempsey says. "You go from junior, where you're the go-to guy, playing the power-play, penalty-kill, last five minutes and first five minutes of every period, to getting three or four shifts a whole game in the NHL or being a healthy scratch. That's tough on a 19-year-old kid."

Brewer played in 63 games as an NHL rookie for the Islanders in 1998–99, compiling 11 points, 89 hits and 32 blocked shots. But the following year he was forced to split time between the struggling NHL club and its Lowell, Massachusetts American Hockey League farm team. He played only 26 games in the NHL that season and failed to score once.

"We weren't a great team in New York," Brewer recalls, thinking back on the frustration of his early days in the NHL. "And when you're in that situation as a young player, sometimes you try to do too much."

"I think that he lost his confidence a bit," Frank Brewer says. "He had a couple of injuries and didn't get back into the swing of things. But he went down to the minors and put his nose to the grindstone and tried to turn things around."

What really seemed to turn everything around for Eric Brewer didn't happen on the ice, however. On June 24, 2000, he was traded to the Oilers in a deal that sent Edmonton defenceman Roman Hamrlik to New York. Brewer was returning to Canada and, most importantly for his family, back to the West where they would be able to see him play in

TEEING UP A TRADE

The biggest turning point in the hockey career of defenceman Eric Brewer might have actually occurred on the golf course. Eric and his father, Frank, were playing the ninth hole of The Dunes in Kamloops when one of the pro shop staff came running out to tell Eric he had an important phone call waiting. It was June 24, 2000 — NHL draft day — and Brewer had been traded from the New York Islanders to the Edmonton Oilers, setting in motion his rise to Olympian and All-Star status.

person much more often. The Brewers were ecstatic. Eric would be playing just an eight-hour drive away from their home in Kamloops.

"I had heard some rumours during the summer, but until you actually get traded you just take them with a grain of salt," Brewer says. "But everyone thought going to Edmonton was great."

Everyone was right. The change in scenery seemed to do wonders for Brewer's game. Going from the Islanders, then one of the league's doormats, to the young, swift-skating Oilers and one of the league's best ice surfaces at Skyreach Centre seemed to be just what he needed. The young blueliner was given plenty of ice time and Oilers assistant coach Charlie Huddy took the time to show Brewer some of the finer points of playing defence in the NHL, such as how to better position himself in his own zone and how to better use his stick. It also helped his psyche that the Oilers were at least contenders for a playoff spot.

"WHEN I FOUND OUT I was on the Olympic team, it was like: 'Wow, this is probably the best team in the world. This is it!'" —Eric Brewer

"I felt like the hockey management in Edmonton was a lot more inclined toward the hockey than they were toward the business end of it," says Frank Brewer.

Since the trade, Eric Brewer has evolved into one of the best young defencemen in the league. Dempsey says Brewer's growth in the NHL has mirrored what he was able to do in Prince George. Once he got comfortable, that is. "He got a big break getting dealt to Edmonton," Dempsey adds.

Brewer played in 77 games with the Oilers in the 2000–1 season, recording an impressive seven goals and 14 assists while leading the team with a plus-15, the first time in his NHL career he had finished on the plus side of the ledger. He also added 162 hits and, during his first appearance in the NHL playoffs, collected six points in six games.

The next season, Brewer matched that seven-goal total while earning 18 assists.

"I think the trade just gave me a chance to reflect and realize that things are never as bad as you might think, that you just can't be too hard on yourself," Brewer says. "It was a clean start."

It was also a launching pad for Brewer to rocket his NHL career to another level. Not only did he become a defensive stalwart for the Oilers in short order, he also earned a surprise spot on the Canadian Olympic team blue line during his second season in Edmonton. Brewer was chosen as a member of the Canadian side that captured the gold medal in Salt Lake City. He even scored twice during six games in the Olympic tournament.

The invitation to play for Canada came less than a year after Brewer represented his country at the 2001 world championship tournament in Germany. "I didn't have any thought about playing in the Olympics at the time I accepted the invitation to play in the worlds," he says. "I hadn't been to a world championship since I was in junior [in 1998 at Helsinki] and I was very excited about that chance."

Brewer played well enough to land an invitation to the subsequent Olympic training camp. Once he got that far, he knew he had a shot at representing Canada in the world winter sports showcase. He didn't let that opportunity slip away.

"When I found out I was on the Olympic team," he says, "it was like: 'Wow, this is probably the best team in the world. This is it!'"

The Olympic experience was also a huge thrill for Frank and Anna Brewer, who made the trip to Salt Lake City to watch their son's finest moment as a hockey player.

"It really came as a surprise," Frank says. "I didn't think they would take any young kids on the team and let them play. That was an awesome thing to see. I had never been to an Olympics before. It really is electrifying, the crowds, the families, the athletes."

Playing in the Olympics is the biggest accomplishment of Brewer's hockey career. He felt a surge of confidence returning to the Oilers after the experience, a far cry from just a couple of years earlier on Long Island when his NHL career seemed to be flagging. He went on to represent Canada again at the 2002 world championships in Sweden and he carried that momentum into the 2002–3 season, accumulating career highs of eight goals, 21 assists and 29 points and making the Western Conference team for the NHL All-Star Game in south Florida. While some in Edmonton were concerned with his minus-11 showing for the season, the worst of any Oilers defenceman, Brewer logged nearly 25 minutes a game in ice time. He finished with a strong playoff, recording four points and going plus-1 in a six-game series loss against the Dallas Stars.

After the Oilers were eliminated in the first round of the playoffs, Brewer again suited up for Team Canada at the 2003 worlds in Helsinki, his third straight appearance in the tournament. Obviously international hockey — particularly the 2002 Olympics — has benefited his development.

"The players on that Olympic team were mainly veterans and they were all good guys," Frank Brewer says. "Any young guy has got to get something out of that experience."

That experience has helped Brewer grow into a top-flight NHL defenceman, perhaps the most difficult position for a young player to master in the world's best hockey league. Maybe he didn't want to be on the blue line initially way back in minor hockey, but most people would agree now that Eric Brewer and the blue line are a pretty nice fit.

"Definitely, it's the toughest position to learn," he says. "You're the last line of defence out there. Any mistakes you make are going to be magnified because the other team is going to be alone on your goalie.

"But I'm feeling comfortable out there. I'm more confident, I'm making better decisions and making plays that I couldn't have when I was younger." HYS

WN.
48
STON
SABRES

DANIEL BRIERE #48

BUFFALO SABRES • CENTRE

Height: 5-10 Weight: 181 Born: October 06, 1977 – Gatineau, PQ

Season	Team	GP	G	A	TP	PIM	+/-	Shots	Pct
1997–1998	Coyotes	5	1	0	1	2	1	4	25.0
1998–1999	Coyotes	64	8	14	22	30	-3	90	8.88
1999–2000	Coyotes	13	1	1	2	0	0	9	11.11
2000–2001	Coyotes	30	11	4	15	12	-2	43	25.58
2001–2002	Coyotes	78	32	28	60	52	6	149	21.47
2002–2003	Coyotes	68	17	29	46	50	-21	142	11.97
2002–2003	Sabres	14	7	5	12	12	1	39	17.94
NHL Totals		272	77	81	158	158	-18	476	16.17

There is much more to the average NHL player than the physical package of muscle and sweat fans see streaking down the ice. Behind every young player who manages to reach the big leagues are parents, coaches, teachers, brothers and sisters who have helped them along the way.

Behind Daniel Briere, there is a bigger crowd than most. He and wife Sylvie have three boys under the age of five — Caelan, Carson and baby Cameron. Counting dad, all they need is a goalie and the Brieres would be able to ice their own family hockey team.

Daniel and Sylvie have been a couple for nearly a decade, ever since they were high school sweethearts in Gatineau, Quebec. And although Sylvie doesn't profess to be any sort of hockey expert, she has had an awful lot to do with her husband's success.

"I have to give her a lot of credit," Daniel says. "She's had some tough times with me being away from home and her having to deal with the kids all by herself. When I'm on the road with the team, she's really good at making me feel like everything at home is under control."

Sylvie has also helped Daniel deal with the often frustrating path of professional hockey. Unlike a chosen few young players whose ascension to the NHL is quick and permanent, the diminutive centre has had to work hard, be patient and constantly prove himself.

Briere spent parts of four seasons in the minor leagues, forcing himself, Sylvie and the kids to bounce between Springfield, Massachusetts, site of the NHL Coyotes' American Hockey League farm club, Phoenix and their hometown of Gatineau. But after a breakthrough season in 2001–2, he signed a two-year deal with Phoenix that provided the family with a sense of certainty.

SPEAKING OF STICKS
It might sound strange, but Daniel Briere likes to talk to his hockey sticks. Briere began speaking to his sticks on the bench during his junior days in Quebec and he hasn't stopped since. He keeps three or four sticks at the ready and rewards them with a rest when they help him earn a goal or an assist. "People will think I'm crazy," he says. "But I talk a lot to my sticks. And if they do the job, I tell them I'm going to give them a break." No word yet on whether they answer back.

"For us, this year is the first year that's actually secure," Sylvie Briere said midway through the 2002–3 season. "The security is very nice, especially with the boys being older."

Nevertheless, hockey season remains a hectic time for the Brieres. Daniel is on the road for 41 regular-season games each winter, leaving Sylvie to make sure things are running smoothly at home. But with Briere being in the NHL full-time, the family now at least has a constant base during the winter. In the summer they return to their home in Gatineau, just across the Ottawa River from the Canadian capital.

A steady job in the big leagues also means professional satisfaction for Briere, who has had to dig deep to overcome doubts about his size and his defensive abilities.

"It was very frustrating," Daniel recalls of his time in the minors. "That was one of the things that motivated me to make the NHL — to be able to spend more time with them. It's really hard to spend that much time away from your family. It's tough being away from your children when they're very young."

Daniel Briere was very young himself when he first took to the ice. His parents, Bob and Constance, flooded the backyard in Gatineau and had their boy on skates by the time he was just two years old. As he grew up, he spent six or seven days a week during winter in the backyard or at the community arena. Young Daniel took to hockey right away. There was never a need to coax him into getting up for 6 a.m. practices, says Bob Briere, an insurance adjuster who played at the junior A level himself as a youngster.

Daniel began playing tyke hockey at age seven, skating with and against kids as old as nine. By the time his second season rolled around, as an eight-year-old, he was already dominating everybody. "My dad was always involved with hockey and got me out on skates really early and I'm really grateful he did," Daniel says.

Through minor hockey, he was continually the top scorer on his team. "I was always the offensive guy on every team I played on growing up," he says. "But I was always the smallest, also."

As a result he grew up watching smaller players, taking cues from NHLers such as Mats Naslund, Theo Fleury and Doug Gilmour — players who had managed to flourish in the NHL despite their size.

Still, that stigma — Briere stands five foot 10 and weighs 181 pounds, small for any position in the NHL — would dog him throughout his minor career. It would also motivate him. "People said I was too small at every level," he says. "My goal was to prove them wrong. In a sense that was an advantage for me."

Briere wasn't drafted by a single Quebec Major Junior Hockey League team when he was a bantam. So instead he played another year of midget AAA and led Gatineau to a third-place finish in the Air Canada Cup national championship, winning the tournament scoring title. Junior teams certainly took notice then and Briere was a first-round pick among Quebec midget players, going to the Drummondville Voltigeurs.

All those who thought he couldn't play junior quickly had their eyes opened as Briere, then just five foot eight and 155 pounds, piled up impressive numbers for Drummondville. He had 123 points, including 51 goals, winning QMJHL offensive rookie-of-the-year honours. The next season he racked up 163 points, including 67 goals and 96 assists, in 67 games to lead the entire Canadian major junior circuit in scoring.

"I didn't really believe growing up that I was ever going to play in the NHL," Briere says. "But at the end of my first year of junior, that's when I first realized that I might have what it takes to make a career out of hockey."

Others thought so, too. The Phoenix Coyotes selected him in the first round, 24th overall, of the 1996 NHL entry draft. And after his final season in Drummondville, he managed to play five games in the NHL during the 1997–98 season.

Most of that season, however, was spent in Springfield, where Briere quickly shone for the AHL Falcons, scoring 36 goals and adding 56 assists to make the first all-star team and capture the Dudley "Red" Garrett Memorial Trophy as the AHL's rookie of the year.

It seemed Briere was on the fast track to a permanent spot with the Coyotes. He made the NHL team at the following training camp and played in 64 games for Phoenix that season. "For me, it was just the way it was supposed to be," Briere says.

Thing were going well — until the Coyotes' final game of the preseason, that is. Briere was on the ice at the Arrowhead Pond when his feet were kicked out from under him by Anaheim defenceman Ruslan Salei. Briere's head thudded against the ice as he fell, knocking him unconscious and leaving him in convulsions. He had to be carried from the ice and he spent his 21st birthday in the hospital.

Daniel missed two games due to the concussion but, in retrospect, he should have sat out longer. The lingering headaches and fogginess kept him from regaining the form. "I started struggling," he says. "I lost confidence in myself. I wasn't scoring and I lost the fun of the game. I wasn't the same player after that."

He finished the NHL season with eight goals and 22 points, but also spent 13 games with Springfield and one with Las Vegas of the International Hockey League that winter. The next year, the Coyotes had Briere start the season in the minors and he made it up to the big club for only 13 games, collecting just two NHL points. He had tried to get stronger by putting on upper body weight, but had ignored his legs. As a result, he lost a step on the ice and struggled even more. "I was making excuses, starting to blame other people," Briere recalls.

While that was his low mark as a pro, he says it also led to a turning point. "I think I grew up then. I spent that third year as a pro playing in the minors. I told myself: 'I can play in the NHL, but I have to make it happen.'"

In his fourth year in the Phoenix organization, Briere battled through training camp with groin and hip flexor problems. He was again sent to Springfield, but this time he went down with a new attitude. He went to see Falcons coach Marc Potvin and told him he was ready to be a complete player, to play in every situation. "He gave me the chance to do all that."

Springfield Falcons general manager Bruce Landon says Briere needed to add more grit to his game. "Early on in his time here, when games got physical, teams would take liberties with Danny," Landon recalls. "I think it threw him off his game. But I think now he's learned how to play through that."

Halfway through that fourth pro season, Briere was called up by the Coyotes after posting 46 points in 30 AHL games. This time he capitalized, recording 11 goals and four assists in 30 games with the NHL club. "That was the last time I was in the minors," he says.

The following season marked Daniel Briere's breakthrough as an NHL scorer. He piled up 32 goals and 28 assists in 78 games with the Coyotes, finishing plus-6 on the season and averaging nearly 16 minutes of ice time per game in 2001–02. His shooting percentage of

"PEOPLE SAID I WAS too small at every level. My goal was to prove them wrong. In a sense that was an advantage for me."
—Daniel Briere

21.5 was the best in the entire NHL. Briere ended the season strongly, scoring 15 goals and adding 19 assists over the final 32 games. He was rewarded with a two-year deal worth $1.35 million US, providing the stability for his young family that had previously eluded him.

Sylvie Briere is not a major hockey fan herself. Her brother, Sebastien, played junior against Daniel in Quebec and she spent a lot of time in rinks as a girl. "By the time I was 16, hockey was old news to me," she laughs. "Hockey is definitely not my top priority." When the couple was married in Gatineau in 2000, only two hockey players attended the wedding. "I wanted it to be our wedding, not a hockey event," she says.

Sylvie does try to attend every home game, but until the most recent season she didn't watch many of her husband's road games on television. "I don't have to watch games," she says. "I'll know by the tone of his voice on the phone after the game how it went."

Pro hockey still brings some uncertainty to any NHL family. Even regular NHLers are subject to dramatic changes through things such as injuries, slumps or trades. That fact was driven home to Briere on March 11, 2003, when he was dealt from the Coyotes to the Buffalo Sabres for Chris Gratton. Over 14 games with the Sabres to finish the season, he posted an impressive seven goals and 12 points playing on Buffalo's top line with Jochen Hecht and J. P. Dumont. For the full season, Briere finished with 24 goals and 58 points.

The trade to Buffalo brought the Brieres closer to home and family in Gatineau and to more of a traditional hockey town. At least for now.

"When you're in the NHL, you never know," Sylvie says. "But it doesn't matter where he is, as long as we're together." HYS

MIKE COMRIE #89

EDMONTON OILERS • CENTRE

Height: 5-9 Weight: 178 Born: September 11, 1980 – Edmonton

Season	Team	GP	G	A	TP	PIM	+/-	Shots	Pct
2000–2001	Oilers	41	8	14	22	14	6	62	12.90
2001–2002	Oilers	82	33	27	60	45	16	170	19.41
2002–2003	Oilers	69	20	31	51	90	-18	170	11.76
NHL Totals		192	61	72	133	149	4	402	15.17

All night long he tossed and turned, and when it was time for breakfast Mike Comrie didn't feel much like eating. It was the biggest day of his life and the only thing the 20-year-old had on his mind was hockey. Food and sleep could certainly wait.

It was December 30, 2000, and Comrie was about to live the dream of nearly every Canadian kid who has laced on a pair of skates. Not only was he going to play his first game in the NHL, he was also going to skate onto the ice at Edmonton's Skyreach Centre wearing the white sweater of his beloved hometown Oilers.

That afternoon, Comrie took part in a press conference to announce his signing. He was so excited that he couldn't even think about a pregame meal or a nap. He made his way down to the dressing room, was issued three sticks, his brand new equipment and an Oilers jersey with his name on the back. He hadn't even practised with the team, yet minutes later he would be skating through the huge mock oil derrick and onto the same ice that Wayne Gretzky, Mark Messier, Jari Kurri and Paul Coffey had graced before him.

"It was more of a blur than anything else — the whole day was a whirlwind experience," Comrie recalls. "It was pretty overwhelming. It was something I'll always cherish. I mean, I'd gone to so many Oiler games — even when I was playing junior in [suburban] St. Albert I went to watch them.

"It was incredible. I felt like a fan who had just won a lottery and my prize was to play in an NHL game."

Certainly nobody could have scripted things much better for Mike Comrie. The hometown kid made his Oilers debut that night in a 3-2 overtime win over the Montreal Canadiens. In the stands were his father Bill, stepmother Roxanne, sister Cathy and brothers Paul, Eric and Ty. "We were all pretty nervous," Bill Comrie recalls. "It was a great thrill, a wonderful thing for the whole family. The hoopla was so big."

And for good reason. Mike Comrie, the Edmonton boy, had been lighting it up with the Western Hockey League's Kootenay Ice, leading the entire major junior league in scoring at the Christmas break. The Oilers had to sign Comrie before January 1, 2001 or they wouldn't be able to place him on their active roster for the rest of the regular season. More pressing yet for the Oilers, a loophole in the NHL rules meant Comrie was slated to become an unrestricted free agent on July 1 if Edmonton failed to sign him before then. The drama dragged on until the second-last day of the year, when Comrie inked a deal with the team on which it seems he was destined to play.

Comrie was informed of the contract the night before in Cranbrook. He had already racked up 39 goals and 40 assists in just 37 games with the Ice. Expectations in Edmonton were high over the arrival of the 20-year-old, whose older brother Paul was also a forward in the Oilers organization. Some wondered if the pressure would be too great.

"I FELT LIKE A FAN who had just won a lottery and my prize was to play in an NHL game." — Mike Comrie on his emotional debut with the Edmonton Oilers

Right from that first night, however, Mike Comrie has managed to live up to those expectations and, more often than not, exceed them. He finished his rookie half season with eight goals and 14 assists in 41 games. And he practically cemented his local-boy-makes-good reputation by scoring the game-winner in overtime victory over the Dallas Stars in the 2001 playoffs.

The following season, Comrie truly arrived as an NHL star with 33 goals and 27 assists in 82 games. Not only that, but he went an impressive plus-6 while stepping into the Oilers' No. 1 centre role after the departure of free agent Doug Weight to the St. Louis Blues.

Many have been surprised with the production of Comrie, who stands just five foot nine and weighs 178 pounds. Those aren't the sort of physical stats that tend to catch the eyes of scouts in the bigger-is-better world of pro hockey.

But Comrie has dealt with the size issue all his life and dealt with it well. Even as a three-year-old playing in his first organized prenovice hockey league in Edmonton with players three or four years older, he never had much of a problem matching up to bigger bodies.

Maybe that's because he got such an early start in the game. Mike was just two when Bill, a former NHL prospect himself, began taking the youngster out on their backyard rink, which Mike and Paul helped their dad create with buckets and hoses each winter. In organized minor hockey Bill also was always on the ice with his boys, coaching their teams until Mike had reached the peewee level. Mike's mother, Theresea, died of cancer in 1991, and the family is extremely close. "My dad is the reason I am where I am today," Mike says.

Maybe, too, Mike Comrie's success has a lot to do with the well-documented Comrie family work ethic. A standout junior forward for the Moose Jaw Canucks and Edmonton

Oil Kings, Bill Comrie signed with the Chicago Black Hawks as a 16-year-old. But he had to quit hockey at age 19 to help support his family after his own father died. Bill Comrie took over the small family furniture business in Edmonton, eventually parlaying it into the 70-store, Canada-wide Brick chain, which in 2003 was expected to surpass $1 billion in sales. "It doesn't matter how small your company is, you can't underestimate its potential," Bill Comrie once told an Edmonton Chamber of Commerce luncheon, a comment that might just as well apply to son Mike's hockey career.

Whatever the primary reason for dark-haired, steely-eyed Mike Comrie's NHL success, his love for the game came early and honestly. His father remembers Mike, hockey pants to his ankles, suiting up for his very first games as a three-year-old. "He was always an excellent skater," Bill recalls. "He actually started skating on roller skates when he was just one."

He was also always smaller than most other players on the ice. But that never seemed to bother Mike, not even when he played well ahead of his peer group. "For Mike, the other players were always bigger," Bill laughs now. "They still are."

Mike never paid much attention to the size difference. He and Paul spent hours skating and playing shinny and concentrating on developing the skills that would one day see them both skate in the NHL. "I think every kid in Canada growing up in that era, that was just the normal thing to do," Mike says. "My brother and I played hockey every day and it just became part of our lives."

Mike did get some early exposure to professional sports that wasn't exactly routine, however. His father always had a strong connection to sports, particularly hockey. Bill was for a time part owner of the San Diego Gulls of the American Hockey League as well as the Los Angeles Ice Dogs of the International Hockey League. He was also owner of the Canadian Football League's B.C. Lions during part of the 1990s. But the Comrie family's first love was always the Oilers. Since day 1, they had season tickets to the team, and Bill's business contacts and friendship with former Oilers owner Peter Pocklington allowed his boys access to the Edmonton dressing room.

Mike can remember visiting the Oilers room as early as age five. He remembers well his friendships with Wayne Gretzky, Mark Messier and other Oilers of the time. He and Paul would sometimes go to practices and Gretzky would often swing around to the Comries' West Edmonton house, pick up the boys and take them to the rink. Sometimes they would fool around on the ice with the players after practice.

"I was very fortunate being around guys who were playing in the NHL and seeing what it took to get there, seeing how hard they worked when they were there," Mike says. "You become a better player when you see things like that."

From the beginning young Mike Comrie displayed a knack for skating, handling the puck, and making big plays. He played with older kids in organized leagues until peewee, when body contact became part of the game. Then he reverted to his own age group. "I was a smaller player," he laughs. "I didn't want to get killed."

At 16 he made the lineup of the Tri-City Americans of the Western Hockey League. But after careful consideration he decided against the jump to major junior, where he might well have had a difficult time physically at that age. Instead, Comrie opted to remain at home, playing for the St. Albert Saints of the tier 2 Alberta Junior Hockey League, a smaller circuit where size wasn't as much of a factor and the calibre of play was still good. He dominated at that level, amassing 78 points and earning AJHL rookie-of-the-year honours. He followed that up with a league-best 60 goals and 78 assists the next season. Along the way, he was AJHL MVP and Canadian junior A hockey player of the year.

Those achievements led to Comrie being vigourously recruited by U.S. college teams and he eventually opted for the storied University of Michigan Wolverines and their head coach, former NHL star Red Berenson. "Mike was so young-looking and so small-looking, he looked liked he could be the stick boy on the team," Berenson recalls of Comrie's arrival as a freshman at Michigan. "But once he got the puck, you could see why this kid was special. He had the puck on a string."

At Michigan, Comrie picked up right where he had left off in St. Albert. In his first year of college hockey he had 19 goals and 44 points in 42 games and earned conference rookie-of-the-year honours as well as an all-conference selection. It was enough to prompt his hometown Oilers to make him the 91st overall pick in the 1999 NHL draft.

BAUER
OILERS
89
EASTON

STEPS TO SUCCESS
University of Michigan coach Red Berenson conducts an annual preseason fitness test for his team. Every fall, his players run the steps of the school's football stadium, going up one aisle and down another. Berenson remembers the drill during Mike Comrie's final year at the school: "By the time we got halfway around, there was one kid who was way out in front of everybody else—Mike Comrie. He separated himself from the rest by two or three rows. It was amazing. He was making a statement that he was ready for the season."

That drove Comrie to work harder than ever. He piled up 24 goals and 35 assists as a sophomore for Michigan, making the all-conference first team and the National Collegiate Athletic Association West second All-American team. He was fifth in NCAA scoring and a finalist for the prestigious Hobey Baker Award.

Once again, however, Comrie was on the move. Although he enjoyed college life immensely at Michigan, he left the Wolverines in the summer after his sophomore season to sign with the Kootenay Ice of the Western Hockey League. It was time to make the step to the more physical WHL, where Comrie knew he could prove his value to anybody who still thought he was too small to be an impact NHL player. The move also took advantage of a loophole in the NHL rules that allowed college players who had previously been drafted to become unrestricted free agents one year after leaving school. Going to Kootenay would allow Comrie to improve his bargaining position and control his own NHL destiny.

His stay with the Ice wasn't long. With the NHL loophole forcing his hand, Edmonton Oilers' general manager Kevin Lowe had to make a decision. "I had always wanted to play in Edmonton, like every kid who grew up in the city," Comrie says. "But I wasn't sure what the Oilers would do."

On December 30, 2000, the Oilers agreed to a three-year deal that would ultimately be worth about $10 million US, setting the stage for the biggest night in Mike Comrie's young life.

Bill Comrie remembers watching with pride as Mike's dream was realized. Just over a year earlier, he had watched with similar emotion as his eldest son, Paul, debuted with the Oilers on the same night the NHL team retired Wayne Gretzky's sweater. "Parents [of talented hockey players] usually think they know that their kid is going to play in the NHL," Bill says. "But you never really know until it happens."

For Bill Comrie, it has happened twice. The only imperfection in the story line is the fact that concussion problems forced Paul to retire after just 15 NHL games and before he had the chance to play alongside his younger brother in an Oilers uniform. Paul was a promising young player in the Oilers' system when he was felled by an elbow during a game with Edmonton's farm team, the Hamilton Bulldogs, on January 7, 2000. After attempting to come back, he finally retired in August 2001 at age 24 because he was suffering from exercise-induced post-concussion syndrome.

Nevertheless, it was Paul who helped convince Mike to sign in Edmonton, culminating a dream the two shared as kids growing up in the city. The brothers are extremely close and now share a house in west Edmonton. Paul has since turned his attention to the family business but he still provides advice and a shoulder to lean on. "Mike and Paul are best friends," Bill Comrie says. "The hardest part is that they weren't able to play together."

Mike Comrie has carried the family name proudly. He has become one of the Oilers' biggest stars, despite being one of the league's smallest players.

"My whole life, I've always had to do things differently because of my size, and that's made me a stronger player, I think," he says. "Everybody as a player has their downfalls and it's what you do to overcome them that makes you a better player."

Comrie had never missed a hockey game due to injury until the 2002–3 season, when he broke his right thumb while blocking a shot from the point by Dan McGillis of the Sharks in January. The injury caused him to miss 13 games. Prior to that he had played in 156 consecutive NHL games and he didn't like the interruption. "It's killing me," he admitted during his recovery period.

It also seemed to kill his momentum for the remainder of his third season as an Oiler. Comrie scored just six times during the final 29 games after returning. He finished the regular season with 20 goals and 31 assists but was a career-worst minus-18 for the year and didn't resemble the player Edmonton fans have come to love. It didn't get any better in the postseason, either, as Comrie managed only one goal.

"It's one of those things you put behind you, move on, and do everything you can to become better the next year," he told the Edmonton *Journal* shortly before joining Team Canada for the world championships in Helsinki.

For the most part, however, Mike Comrie's hockey career has been a lesson in how determination can overcome a size deficit. It has read like a Hollywood script: Hometown hero uses hard work and skill to become a star in the same city in which he grew up. Comrie can't imagine it turning out a different way.

"Trades are part of the NHL," he says. "But for me, at least at this stage of my career, putting on another team's sweater would be like putting on the uniform of a different country." HYS

ITECH
GABORIK
EASTON

MARIAN GABORIK #10

MINNESOTA WILD • WINGER

Height: 6-1 Weight: 183 Born: February 14, 1982 – Trencin, Slovakia

Season	Team	GP	G	A	TP	PIM	+/-	Shots	Pct
2000–2001	Wild	71	18	18	36	32	-6	179	10.05
2001–2002	Wild	78	30	37	67	34	0	221	13.57
2002–2003	Wild	81	30	35	65	46	12	280	10.71
NHL Totals		230	78	90	168	112	6	680	11.47

Minnesota Wild assistant general manager Tom Thompson remembers the first time he laid eyes on Marian Gaborik. It was at the Keystone Centre in Brandon, Manitoba, in December 1998. Gaborik was a 16-year-old, playing left wing for Slovakia in the world junior hockey championships. At the time, Thompson was a scout for the Edmonton Oilers and Gaborik wasn't particularly high on his priority list.

"When you're scouting at those things, you're so focused on players for the upcoming National Hockey League draft that you don't really look at the underage guys," Thompson recalls. "But I had a hard time keeping my eyes off him. Marian really registered as a 16-year-old."

Marian Gaborik made almost everybody sit up and take notice during that world tournament with his combination of youth, eye-catching bursts of speed and magical puck-handling ability, scoring three goals in six games as he helped the Slovaks capture a surprising bronze medal. "The speed combined with the puck skills is what really caught my eye," Thompson remembers.

First impressions usually stick with people, and pro hockey scouts are no different. Tom Thompson certainly didn't forget Gaborik after Thompson was hired away from the Oilers to help build the expansion Minnesota Wild from scratch the next fall.

The Wild weren't scheduled to enter the NHL until the 2000–1 season, which gave general manager Doug Risebrough and his team of scouts — led by Thompson — an entire year to prepare for their inaugural season.

The Wild knew they would pick No. 4, at worst, in the 2000 NHL entry draft. And Marian Gaborik was high on their list of prospects as they tried to determine who would be the franchise's first-ever selection. "I saw him a lot over that year," Thompson says.

He certainly did. Thompson scouted Gaborik at the following world junior tournament in northern Sweden and he also visited the youngster in his hometown of Trencin, Slovakia, a picturesque city of nearly 59,000 close to the borders of Poland, Austria and

MULTI-DIMENSIONAL MARIAN

As a youngster in Slovakia, Marian Gaborik didn't play summer hockey or attend hockey schools but he did enjoy plenty of other activities. While growing up he also sculpted, drew and painted, played soccer and tennis and competed in track and field — not surprisingly, as a sprinter.

the Czech Republic that is overlooked by the 11th-century Trencin Castle.

Thompson watched Gaborik more than hold his own against men in the Slovakian Elite League as a 17-year-old playing with Dukla-Trencin, a club that has produced a long list of NHLers including Marian Hossa, Pavol Demitra, Ziggy Palffy and Miroslav Satan. Thompson even visited Gaborik's home, meeting the player's older brother, parents and grandmother. "I wanted to get a real feel for him off the ice," Thompson says.

What impressed the veteran scout most was Gaborik's maturity. Thompson discovered that Marian had finished high school early and learned to speak English in order to prepare himself for professional hockey in North America. Gaborik was the only member of his family who spoke English at the time and the youngster acted as translator when Thompson visited the family home. The Wild scout was impressed during the visit, observing a well-disciplined setting with plenty of love and mutual support.

"We were pretty concerned about taking an Eastern European in the first four of the draft," Thompson admits now. "We had to know what he was all about. We had to get a feel for how this guy would play after you paid him a lot of money."

Thompson and the Wild were quickly satisfied that Gaborik, whose father had a small business making furniture by hand in Trencin, was well grounded off the ice. But they had to be just as sure that he could develop into their kind of player on the ice. Thompson read hundreds of scouting reports that year, some of which described Gaborik as "a typical one-dimensional European player." But what Thompson saw with his own eyes was much different. He recognized that Gaborik had the potential to be a complete player in the NHL. Gaborik killed penalties with a vengeance and "he backchecked so hard, he was almost spearing guys."

Gaborik was also putting up some impressive numbers in the Slovakian league, finishing with 25 goals and 46 points in 50 games during his second season for Dukla-Trencin, despite the fact that he was still a boy playing against men.

Doug Risebrough saw Gaborik play in person only once during that long lead-up to the expansion team's first draft. But Risebrough was impressed with Gaborik's willingness to work hard as a fourth-liner with the Slovakian national team during a tournament in Switzerland.

In the end, the Wild felt comfortable enough to take Gaborik with their first-ever draft pick, selecting the speedster third overall in the 2000 draft behind Boston University goaltender Rick DiPietro, who went No. 1 to the New York Islanders, and forward Dany Heatley of the University of Wisconsin, chosen second by the Atlanta Thrashers. To say the pick has paid off handsomely is sort of like saying Minnesotans like their hockey.

"He's a guy who carries us," veteran Wild centre Cliff Ronning says of his young linemate. "When Marian plays his best, he's definitely got one or two goals in him or a lot of chances. He's young and he's getting better. Only certain guys can go a hundred miles an hour and make a great play or deke a goalie and he's one of those guys who has that — very much like [Pavel] Bure and [Alexander] Mogilny."

Gaborik joined Minnesota the September after he was drafted and wasted no time making an impact. Although he had to adjust to new rules — there is no red line in European hockey — a much more physical style of play and the smaller North American ice surface, his performance in training camp forced the Wild to keep him in the NHL rather than assign him to their American Hockey League farm team in Houston. In the Wild's first season, he had 18 goals and 18 assists in 71 games on the wing. "The only thing that surprised me is how quickly he did it," Thompson says.

The arrival of Marian Gaborik coincided with the return of the NHL to Minnesota. It was important for the Wild to have such a promising young player as they began their new love affair with hockey-crazy Minnesotans, who had lost their former team in 1993 when the North Stars relocated to Dallas. The dashing rookie became the symbol of hope for the team as he tallied the Wild's first exhibition goal, scored the franchise's first regular-season goal at Anaheim in his very first NHL game, and also recorded the team's first game-winning goal. Gaborik led Minnesota in points and shots and was among the top NHL rookies in a number of offensive categories that season.

His ability to speak English — improved daily by a passion for watching movies — hastened his adaptation to a new country and culture. A visit from his mother, who stayed for a month during his rookie season and cooked Slovakian fare for her son, helped tremendously with the transition. "It was a totally different country and style of life and everything, you know," Gaborik says. "It took a little while to get used to it."

He followed up his rookie campaign with a remarkable breakthrough sophomore season, registering 30 goals and 37 assists in 78 games, leading to a spot in the NHL's mid-season Young Guns game at the Staples Center in Los Angeles.

But it was in his third season that he truly arrived as a star, turning in a number of highlight-reel plays en route to a 30-goal, 35-assist campaign and leaving fans, players and coaches to wonder just how dominant he could become. Though his point total fell by two from the previous season, Gaborik managed 280 shots, 59 more than in his second year. But perhaps the biggest indicator of his maturity as a player was the fact that he finished with a plus-12 rating on the season and helped the Wild go deep into the playoffs.

On October 26, 2002, Gaborik served up a six-point night at America West Arena in Phoenix, collecting two goals and four assists and prompting Coyotes coach Bob Francis to comment that the only way to stop Gaborik was to lock him in his hotel room.

Less than two months later, the Wild winger made his *Hockey Night in Canada* debut a memorable one by shaking off a charley horse to score three times against Vancouver in a 4-2 Minnesota win at General Motors Place on December 7, giving the slick Slovakian the NHL lead in goals at that juncture.

The performance opened an entire nation's eyes to the talents of Gaborik, particularly the way in which he scored his second goal on a 35-foot rocket of a wrist shot over the outstretched glove hand of Canucks goalie Dan Cloutier after backing down defenceman

Brent Sopel at the blue line. "We all know how good he is, but that one just shows you how much better he's getting," Cloutier marvelled afterward. "Sakic does that all the time."

Joe Sakic was one player Gaborik was drawing comparisons to early in his third NHL season, besides Pavel Bure and Alexander Mogilny. The young Wild star clearly established himself as a player with a "wow" factor. His performance was enough to earn a spot on the Western Conference team for February's NHL All-Star Game in Sunrise, Florida, and he didn't disappoint there, either, winning the skating contest that was part of the Saturday skills competition and scoring a goal during the Sunday afternoon showcase.

Gaborik, however, still seems to much prefer talking about the Wild's collective efforts or about his teammates. When pressed to speak about himself, he has much less to say.

"ONLY CERTAIN GUYS can go a hundred miles an hour and make a great play or deke a goalie and he's one of those guys who has that — very much like Bure and Mogilny."
— Wild captain Cliff Ronning, on teammate Gaborik

He lets the ultraquick release of his deadly accurate shot and the massive thighs built up over hours in the weight room do most of the talking for him. "I tried to work hard over the summer and tried to improve and get stronger and it's been good so far," he says. "I just can't let up."

The remarkable thing about Gaborik is that he has put up such impressive numbers so early as part of a true team concept. Unlike young stars on some other NHL teams, he has not been given free rein to sneak up ice and ignore his defensive responsibilities. Wild head coach Jacques Lemaire, an offensive but responsible forward when he won eight Stanley Cups with the Montreal Canadiens and the brains behind the stingy, defensive New Jersey Devils team that won the Stanley Cup in 1995, expects Gaborik to be a complete player. And on those rare nights when he doesn't have it offensively, the Wild coaching staff expects him to turn in a tenacious defensive game nonetheless.

The thing the Wild brain trust likes about their young, emerging superstar is that he seems eager to learn and improve and displays a solid work ethic. If that continues, the sky is the limit, says Lemaire, because Gaborik's talent makes him a "game-changer."

"This is the most important thing in a kid like that," Lemaire said during Gaborik's third NHL season. "Okay, yes, he has a lot of talent, but if he works he's going to get better. He's still a young guy and he's got a lot to learn."

Better to learn as part of a system such as Lemaire's, say Gaborik's teammates, who seem impressed with the kid's desire to improve as well as his obviously special skills.

It is clear other skaters with the Wild believe they are witnessing something special, the birth of an NHL superstar on the frozen prairie of Minnesota.

Those around the Wild also say they have noticed a maturity in Gaborik since he first arrived from Slovakia as a fresh-faced teenager. He is much more confident with his English, looks reporters in the eye, offers more than one-line answers and has shown glimpses of becoming a leader in the dressing room. These are qualities that Tom Thompson believed he saw on that first visit to Gaborik's home.

Gaborik is still the sort of guy who laughs at jokes rather than telling them himself, Thompson says, but he is also an upbeat player with "a twinkle in his eye" and well liked by teammates.

"How much better can he get?" says Thompson, posing the rhetorical question on a lot of minds across Minnesota. "That's up to him. The pride factor becomes enormous now. Pride has to be the motivating factor. There are a lot of players who are very skilled who simply haven't got it in them to perform at that high level, night after night. He's certainly got the potential to be an elite level of player for a long period of time."

Gaborik is undeniably already a major star in the NHL. His third NHL campaign concluded with an impressive run through the playoffs as the upstart Wild advanced all the way to the Western Conference finals before being swept by the Anaheim Mighty Ducks. Gaborik played a big role in the Minnesota run, scoring nine goals and adding eight assists while going plus-two in 18 playoff games.

And as his fame grows, so do the demands on his time. He is now the story when Minnesota visits just about any NHL city. He is no longer an anonymous European import with loads of potential. While he doesn't seem to enjoy talking about himself, the extra attention doesn't seem to faze him, either.

"I got used to it when I got here to North America and it's the life of a professional athlete," Gaborik says matter-of-factly. "That's how it probably is."

Still, it's a long way from his childhood days in Trencin. Gaborik wasn't yet three years old when his mother taught him how to skate and he watched his older brother Brano, now a scout with the Wild, take up the game before him.

Before long, Gaborik was taking part himself in the Slovakian minor hockey system — which emphasizes skating and skill drills — and he began playing in leagues when he was about nine. "I had good coaches," he says of his minor hockey development. "Everything there was organized, it had some steps and stages."

Gaborik's childhood hockey idol was Peter Bondra, the scoring star of the Washington Capitals, who is also from Slovakia. By the time Marian was a young teenager himself, he was already starting to travel with Slovakian national team programs.

One of Gaborik's key attributes is that he has always been able to perform at high speed, an exhilaration he enjoys off the ice as well. He owns two extremely fast automobiles — a late-model BMW M3 as well as a souped-up 1990 Porsche 911. "I have like over 400 horsepower in both of them," he says, "so it's pretty quick." He also owns a late-model BMW 745, which he uses more for luxury cruising than for pure speed.

The curly-haired Gaborik has certainly used his considerable talents to cruise to a lofty status in the NHL. He has quickly become recognized as one of only a handful of NHL players capable of consistently pulling fans out of their seats with just a single move or a shot.

"Ninety-five per cent of people come to hockey games to be entertained," Thompson says. "Marian can entertain you because he does skilful things at top speed." HYS

SIMON GAGNE #12

PHILADELPHIA FLYERS • LEFT WING

Height: 6-0 Weight: 190 Born: February 29, 1980 – Ste. Foy, PQ

Season	Team	GP	G	A	TP	PIM	+/-	Shots	Pct
1999–2000	Flyers	80	20	28	48	22	11	159	12.57
2000–2001	Flyers	69	27	32	59	18	24	191	14.13
2001–2002	Flyers	79	33	33	66	32	31	199	16.58
2002–2003	Flyers	46	9	18	27	16	20	115	7.82
NHL Totals		274	89	111	200	88	86	664	13.40

As a hockey-crazy 15-year-old growing up in the suburbs of snowy Quebec City, Simon Gagne was among thousands who had their hearts broken on June 21, 1995, when the beloved Nordiques packed up their sticks and pucks and rolls of black tape and made a permanent move to Denver.

Not only was he saying goodbye to his favourite NHL team, but Gagne also had to bid farewell to his favourite player, the smooth-skating Joe Sakic.

"It was really discouraging," Gagne says now, more than eight years later. "The Nordiques were everything for people back then. To lose that team ... well, it's pretty tough to explain. I was a big, big fan. Everybody there was a big, big fan. When you lose your team like that, it's like you lose somebody."

The son of a Quebec City police officer, Gagne had grown up attending a handful of Nordiques games a year and watching them on television as much as possible. Suddenly, in a move that had much more to do with high finance than hockey, they were the Colorado Avalanche and Quebec City was left without an NHL team.

Gagne had grown up on the Nordiques, wearing a Michel Goulet jersey when he was just four years old and then becoming a certified Sakic fan after the smooth centre joined the Nordiques as a 19-year-old in 1988.

"Every time they were on TV, we would watch them," Gagne recalls. "Losing them, it was pretty hard to take."

Happily, though, the hockey gods have had a nice way of evening things out for Simon Gagne. Four years after that devastating blow, he found himself skating in the NHL as a rookie with the Philadelphia Flyers. And less than three years later he was streaking down the left wing on a line with his boyhood hero, Joe Sakic, and helping Team Canada to an Olympic gold medal in Salt Lake City.

Gagne's road to the NHL began early, as it does with so many kids in Quebec. Before he

BAUER

reached the ice for the first time, he was toddling across the carpet in a pair of skates in his parents' suburban Ste-Foy basement. By age two Simon was actually skating, starting first with the aid of a wooden chair on the slippery ice surface and quickly discarding that to go solo. Much of that early skating took place on the 15- by 30-foot backyard rink at the family home.

The youngster came by his skating talent honestly. Pierre Gagne had been a junior hockey standout with the Quebec Aces, good enough to attend a couple of training camps in the 1960s with the expansion Philadelphia Flyers before skating with the New England Blades of the East Coast Hockey League for a season. And Simon's grandfather, Roger, won a Calder Cup with the Cleveland Barons during four seasons in the American Hockey League in the 1940s. So young Simon and his younger brother, Jean-Francois, got an early start in the game and plenty of encouragement and direction along the way.

Losing the Nordiques didn't mean losing his love for hockey. As with many other Quebec kids, the game was in Gagne's blood for good, local NHL franchise or not.

"Where I'm from, if you're not skiing, you have a great chance to be playing hockey, especially when you're a boy," says Gagne, who still lives in Quebec City during the off-season. "Hockey and skiing, that's what kids do up there. I think all my family is interested in hockey."

Like many other talented youngsters, Simon played ahead of his age group, usually skating with and against players two or three years older. Besides hockey, he also played soccer in the off-season until that was replaced by summer hockey just before he hit his teens. Pierre Gagne coached his son as a 9-, 10- and 11-year-old in minor hockey, stressing the importance of defence and backchecking as well as scoring goals.

Simon's minor hockey career included two appearances in the Quebec peewee tournament in 1993 and 1994 and he went on to help the Sainte-Foy Governeurs win the Air Canada Cup national midget championship in Kamloops, British Columbia, in 1996. He was selected 10th in the Quebec Major Junior Hockey League midget draft by the Beauport Harfangs.

At age 16 he posted nine goals and 22 assists in 51 games as a major junior rookie. The next season, when the Harfangs became the Quebec Remparts, he really blossomed, more than doubling his point total (30-39-69) in just two more games and becoming a fan favourite in Quebec City's Le Colisse.

Pierre Gagne had always known his son was a good hockey player. But he didn't even think about the NHL as a possibility until Simon's second year of junior, when several NHL scouts he knew began telling him that his boy was a future pro.

"I knew that the primary quality [to play in the NHL] is skating and his skating is very strong," says Pierre, a police officer for 32 years before retiring a couple of years ago.

That fluid skating, along with the numbers Simon was posting in the QMJHL, prompted the Philadelphia Flyers to select him with the No. 22 pick overall in the 1998 NHL entry draft. The Flyers used their first selection in that draft to take Gagne, acting on the strong recommendation of scout Simon Nolet, a former NHLer who had played junior with Pierre Gagne in Quebec and later attended Flyers training camp with him.

BORN TO SKATE

Pierre Gagne remembers taking his eldest son to the outdoor Gaetan Boucher Skating Oval in Ste-Foy for the first time in December 1976, before Simon had even turned three. There were hundreds of people on the ice that day, enjoying a Christmas skate. "Simon skated with a chair to help him out for maybe 50 feet, then he let the chair go," says his dad. "He did two laps around and he never fell. There were maybe 400 people out on the ice. The people were watching Simon."

Simon was more than happy to go to the Flyers, a fitting destination because of his father's previous connection with the organization. Pierre Gagne attended the draft in Buffalo and recalls it as "a very nice moment" for the family. "I was very happy," he says.

"As a player, you just want to be drafted," Simon says. "It doesn't really matter where you're going. As a kid growing up, watching hockey on TV, you dream about being drafted. It's huge, you can't describe it. But it's just one step. You know you have a lot of stuff to do to actually get to the NHL."

Gagne returned to the Remparts for one more season of junior and his numbers took another astonishing jump. As a 19-year-old, he finished with 50 goals and 70 assists in 61 games to make the QMJHL's second all-star team.

"WHEN MY NAME was called in December, it was a great honour. There were big names on that team, like Lemieux and Sakic. To find my name with them, it was pretty hard to believe."
— Simon Gagne on being selected for the Canadian Olympic team

The Remparts would eventually retire Gagne's No. 12 jersey, making him and former NHL great Guy Lafleur the only two players to ever receive that honour from the junior team.

Still, Gagne says he wasn't sure if he could make it in the NHL until training camp and his first couple of exhibition games with the Flyers. "Before that, I had no clue," he says.

His play as a rookie left little doubt that he was ready to make his mark in the NHL, however. The six-foot, 185-pounder played in 80 games with the Flyers in 1999–2000, scoring 20 times and adding 28 assists to make the NHL's All-Rookie team.

Gagne followed that up with 59 points (27-32) in 11 fewer games during his second season. Despite a shoulder separation that shortened his year, he landed a spot in the NHL All-Star Game at Denver, where he scored a pair of goals, including the winner, playing on a line with Mario Lemieux and Brett Hull.

Gagne's numbers took another jump in his third NHL season as he compiled 33 goals and 33 assists in 79 games, playing mostly on the Flyers' top line with Jeremy Roenick and Mark Recchi. But the highlight of that winter was his selection to the 2002 Canadian Olympic team, a berth that came as a surprise to some.

"That was huge," Simon says. "I had a chance to go to the Olympic team training camp in Calgary in August and just being there, I thought at the time, was great."

He knew the experience would be good for his career and he had previously enjoyed playing for Canada, winning under-18 gold at the 1997 Three Nations tournament and silver at the 1999 world junior championship in Winnipeg, where he finished the tournament with seven goals, including four in one game.

He had no idea just how good the Olympic experience would be, however, until his name was announced by general manager Wayne Gretzky as the youngest member of the Canadian team for the 2002 Salt Lake City Games.

"I thought I was just invited to camp for experience, not to make the team this time," Gagne says. "When my name was called in December, it was a great honour. There were big names on that team, like Lemieux and Sakic. To find my name with them, it was pretty hard to believe. But it was a great honour at the same time."

The announcement also came out of the blue for his father in Quebec City. "It's a big surprise for me," Pierre says now. "He's very young, you know, with no experience. But Wayne Gretzky liked his style."

Gagne didn't disappoint the selectors, enjoying a strong Olympic tournament and helping Canada to a gold medal with one goal and four points in six games. During the final five games at Salt Lake, he played on the same line as Joe Sakic. "It is a dream for him," says his father.

Along with right-winger Jarome Iginla of the Calgary Flames, the line proved potent for Canada. With his father, Pierre, and mother, Nicole, watching from the stands, Gagne assisted once during Canada's 5-2 gold-medal victory over the United States.

"At the end, with the gold medal around my neck, it was amazing to be a part of that team," Simon later told an NHL.com interview session. "Bringing that gold medal back [to Canada] after 50 years is amazing. It was great to be a part of that."

He calls the experience his biggest thrill in hockey so far.

"As a kid, watching Joe Sakic, it was pretty easy to fall in love with his game," Gagne says. "I knew he was great, [but until playing with him at the Olympics] I didn't realize how great."

Simon Gagne's fourth NHL season brought a coaching change for the Flyers. Ken Hitchcock, whose approach to the game is more structured, arrived to replace Bill Barber and Gagne struggled to match his previous numbers. Injuries posed an even greater problem, however. He suffered a concussion in December, followed by a lingering groin injury he first incurred in January. Those injuries limited him to just 46 games and he finished the season with nine goals and 18 assists, the worst point total of his career.

Gagne, who signed a new two-year, $4.7 million US contract before the season began, admits playing under Hitchcock has meant some adjustments on his part. "You have to make sure you don't make mistakes with him," says Gagne, who despite his offensive problems was plus-20 for the 2002–3 season. "I was responsible defensively before, but I'm more defensively responsible now."

During the playoffs, he had four goals and one assist in 13 games as the Flyers reached the Eastern Conference semifinals before being eliminated in six games by the Ottawa Senators.

"I had a tough start to this season," he admits. "You get challenged every year. You're going to have to face the challenges and the tough times. This is only my fourth year in the league and I still have to learn a lot of stuff." HYS

SHERWOOD
PRO7700
SHER-WOOD

MARTIN HAVLAT #9

OTTAWA SENATORS • LEFT WING

Height: 6-1 Weight: 194 Born: April 19, 1981 — Mlada Boleslav, Czech Republic

Season	Team	GP	G	A	TP	PIM	+/-	Shots	Pct
2000–2001	Senators	73	19	23	42	20	8	133	14.28
2001–2002	Senators	72	22	28	50	66	-7	145	15.17
2002–2003	Senators	67	24	35	59	30	20	179	13.40
NHL Totals		212	65	86	151	116	21	457	14.22

With each year he spends in the NHL, Martin Havlat gets a little more comfortable, a little more confident as he dashes down the ice for the Ottawa Senators. Now his coaches would like him to get a little more selfish, too. While that's not considered a virtue in most circles, Havlat could stand being a tad greedier when it comes to putting the puck on net.

"I'm passing too much," the 22-year-old native of the Czech Republic admitted during his third season in the NHL. "I should shoot a little bit more. Instead, I over-pass."

As far as criticisms of young professionals go, it's a minor quibble. The Senators' coaching staff would like their six-foot-one, 190-pound speedster to fire the puck at opposing goaltenders more often, even though he had a career-best 179 shots in 2002–3. And they'd like to see continued defensive growth. But, overall, they certainly have no complaints with the player they selected 26th in the 1999 NHL entry draft.

Martin Havlat has a combination of speed, size and creative moves that makes him one of the most exciting young forwards on one of the NHL's most exciting young teams. His offensive talent allowed him to step straight into the NHL as a 19-year-old from the Czech Republic elite league and he has worked to improve the defensive side of his game since he arrived in the Canadian capital.

"I'm more confident every year," Havlat says. "It's much different than the first year. I know the system now.

"When I first came to Ottawa it was a big difference. The ice is smaller, everything is faster and quicker. There's not as much time to do what you want as there was back home or in Europe. Back there, there is no red line. You just need time to get used to it all."

Havlat didn't need much time at all, really. In his first season in the NHL he immediately put up impressive numbers, scoring 19 goals and 42 points in 73 games. He was NHL rookie of the month for October and tallied his first goal on October 14 against the Toronto Maple Leafs. As a sophomore NHLer, he upped those numbers to 22 goals and 50 points

SHARING THE WEALTH

Thanks to the nearly million-dollar salary he draws with the Ottawa Senators, Martin Havlat has been able to help his family. After his rookie season in the NHL, he bought a house in the Czech Republic for his mother and father. "They have never lived in a house before," he says. "They lived in an apartment. I thought they deserved to have some more space."

while playing in one less game. But the youngster truly seemed to find his stride during his third NHL season when, still just 21 years old, he beat his previous personal-best points totals with 24 goals, 35 assists and 59 points while going an impressive plus-20.

Those numbers came despite a strange year for the Ottawa franchise in which it declared bankruptcy and saw its players miss a paycheque during January while staying near the top of the overall standings all winter. Havlat shrugs off the turmoil, saying it was no distraction for the players.

"We're used to that sort of thing back home," he laughs. "It doesn't affect us on the ice at all."

Havlat comes by his hockey talent honestly. His father, Slava, now in his seventies, played defence in the Czechoslovakian elite league and later became a high-profile coach in his country. Slava Havlat coached his son almost every season until the boy was 16. Martin now wears No. 9 with the Senators because that was the number his father donned as a player.

It was Slava who took Martin skating for the first time when the youngster was about five. At first Martin learned to steady himself with a chair on the ice. Soon, that was no longer necessary.

"I was with my father on the road sometimes and we sometimes skated before practices," Havlat recalls.

Within a year of his first skate, the boy was playing hockey in his hometown of Brno, located in the heart of Europe in the southeast portion of the Czech Republic and the country's second-largest city, with a population of about 380,000.

Even at age six, Martin showed plenty of speed and a flair for the offensive aspects of the game. He admired the way Wayne Gretzky played, even though there wasn't much of an opportunity to watch No. 99 on television. Jaromir Jagr and Patrik Elias were obvious home-country heroes, so Havlat also looked up to them. Swede Peter Forsberg and Canadian Joe Sakic were among the international array of NHLers he admired.

"I was always scoring goals," Havlat says of his earliest hockey days in his homeland. "But lots of guys score goals when they're young."

Not many young players make the sort of jump Havlat did at age 17, however. It was then that he made the move from the junior team in the city of Trinec up to the club's first team in the Czech Republic elite league, also known as the Extraleague. In that initial half season with the Ocelari, playing against seasoned men, Havlat recorded just two goals and five points over 24 games.

That same season, the 17-year-old skated with the Czech Republic entry in an under-18 tournament at Lake Placid, New York. That was the first time Trevor Timmins laid eyes on Martin Havlat.

"He had a good skating style — that's what you could notice about him right away," says Timmins, then a scout with the Senators and now the director of player personnel for the Montreal Canadiens.

"But Martin didn't accomplish much in that first tournament I saw him in. Still, you always have to be careful with European players. Sometimes they don't do their best when it's their first time in North America."

The following season, Havlat's numbers in the Czech Extraleague skyrocketed. As an 18-year-old he piled up 42 points, including 13 goals, in 46 games.

The same winter, Senators scout Andre Savard watched Havlat with interest in February at the Four Nations Cup tournament. Savard liked what he saw. In April, Trevor Timmins again scouted Havlat, this time at the European junior under-18 tournament in Fussen, Germany. And this time it was more than Havlat's skating that stood out for the veteran scout.

"That was in April and the big name at the time for the upcoming draft [among the Czech Republic players] seemed to be Michal Sivek [who eventually went 29th to Tampa Bay]. But I felt Havlat outplayed him there," Timmins said.

"He had good speed, demonstrated good drive. He's the type of player who wants the puck and he had some jam to his game, which you like to see."

The NHL draft that June was held in Boston. Havlat's father's health was failing and wouldn't allow him to travel to the United States for the draft, but his brother, also named Slava, made the trip with Martin.

"It was pretty exciting to be there," Havlat recalls. "But it was just the first step. It doesn't mean you're going to play in the NHL."

Havlat was delighted to go in the first round and he was pleased to go to the Senators. He knew Ottawa had several Czechs and Slovaks in its system and that the Senators favoured a European style of game. "I knew it was a hockey city, too," he said. "But I was just happy I was drafted. I just wanted to play in the NHL."

Timmins, who was one of four Senators brass who were instrumental in drafting Havlat, said Ottawa had the Czech Republic prospect rated highly. "We were excited to get him where we did — at No. 26."

Not only were they pleased with Havlat's hockey skills, they liked the youngster's personality during predraft interviews. "Martin is easy to communicate with," Timmins says. "He listens to you when you talk to him. He asks for advice."

Havlat went to Ottawa that fall with a plan: If he didn't make the Senators, he would return home and play again in the Czech Republic elite league. "The Czech league is one of the best in Europe," he says. "I was not going to play in the [North American] minors."

He didn't have to worry. He didn't spend a single day on the farm but jumped directly into the NHL, despite the obvious cultural adjustment at the tender age of 19.

Havlat was already accustomed to living away from home. During his last two seasons in the Czech Republic he had played at Trinec, about three hours away from Brno. But this was much farther and much different.

"It was a pretty big move," he says. "I didn't know where I was going. I didn't know the language. I didn't know the people here. But I was also pretty excited. I knew I was going to play in the best league in the world. Always that's been the dream of every little guy playing hockey."

Making the transition easier was the presence of several Europeans, including Vaclav Prospal and Radek Bonk of his own country and Marian Hossa of Slovakia, who has since become one of his closest friends on the team. The North American players on the Senators also helped him out. A simple thing — going to the movies — proved to be an effective way to learn the language, too.

"It was a little bit of a weird feeling," he says of suddenly being in Canada. "I was missing home, I was missing friends. I was used to being by myself already, but the first year, especially, around Christmas time, I was a little homesick."

"I KNEW I WAS GOING to play in the best league in the world. Always that's been the dream of every little guy playing hockey." — Havlat, on moving to the NHL from the Czech Republic elite league

He played for his homeland during the 2002 Winter Olympics, at times skating on a line with Jaromir Jagr. In four games in the Olympic tournament, Havlat recorded three goals and one assist.

His family, including his mother, Hana, comes to visit him in Ottawa every year. And Havlat goes back to the Czech Republic every off-season.

Prior to his third NHL season, Havlat returned to Ottawa earlier than usual to work on his strength conditioning, an area in which Timmins said he can still make improvements. "That's the type of commitment you like to see," says the scout.

Defence still isn't the strongest point of Havlat's game but Timmins believes he is learning it as he goes along. And he has the sort of offensive flair that simply can't be taught, the sort of style that led Senators head coach Jacques Martin to say during the 2002–3 season that Havlat at times reminded him of former NHL great Guy Lafleur.

In the 2002–03 post-season, Havlat contributed 11 points — including five goals — and went plus-four to help the Senators advance to the Eastern Conference finals, where they fell in seven games to the New Jersey Devils.

"He's a game-breaking type of player," Timmins says. "Opposing defenceman have to be aware of him whenever he's on the ice."

Timmins, an 11-year NHL scout, said Havlat's big season in 2002–3 didn't come as a shock to him. "I'm not surprised at all. I expected him to improve each and every year. He's still very young. He's got the capability of going a lot further." HVS

DANY HEATLEY #15

ATLANTA THRASHERS • RIGHT WING

Height: 6-3 Weight: 215 Born: January 21, 1981 – Freiburg, Germany

Season	Team	GP	G	A	TP	PIM	+/-	Shots	Pct
2001-2002	Thrashers	82	26	41	67	56	-19	202	12.87
2002-2003	Thrashers	77	41	48	89	58	-8	252	16.27
NHL Totals		159	67	89	156	114	-27	454	14.76

Dany Heatley's hockey career has been on a fast track to superstardom since he was a 15-year-old kid from southwest Calgary. Every step along the way has brought extraordinary success, almost as if his prodigious puck path was somehow preordained. Perhaps it was.

Heatley has followed in the footsteps of his father, Murray, starting as a junior star in his hometown in the southern Alberta foothills, moving on to the University of Wisconsin where he was a standout U.S. collegiate player, and finally on to the professional ranks in the deep south of the United States. But that's where the similarities end, says Murray Heatley, a justifiably proud papa.

"He's a lot better than I ever was," laughed Heatley Sr. during his eldest son's sophomore NHL season, by which time Dany had already arrived as a bona fide star in hockey's toughest league.

Dany Heatley is that rare combination of size — he's six foot three and 215 pounds and still developing — hockey skills, maturity and perseverance that has allowed him to jump into the NHL and excel immediately. The right-winger with the Atlanta Thrashers was the league's rookie of the year in 2001–2 and he followed that up with an MVP performance at the 2003 NHL All-Star Game.

Yes, there is little argument that Heatley has surpassed his father's accomplishments on the ice. But he's quick to point out that he would never have been the player, or the person, he is today without his dad.

"He's definitely been the biggest influence on my career," Heatley says. "We have a great relationship. He knows my game and he knows when I've played well and when I didn't play well, so it's good to hear from him. Growing up, he told me that there is always stuff to work on and that you've just got to keep trying to get better."

It was Murray Heatley who first took his toddler skating at age three on an arena in the southwest of Germany. Young Dany would regularly accompany his dad to the rink in the early '80s as Murray finished out his playing career with ERC Freiburg of Germany's top professional league.

Dany was the first child of Murray and his wife Karin, a German native who met her husband while he was playing overseas. The youngster was born in Freiburg on January 21, 1981, and the Heatley family returned to Calgary not long after Dany celebrated his fourth birthday.

It wasn't obvious from the beginning, however, that he had extraordinary talent for the game. In fact, his father remembers a much different first impression. "When you get to be bigger like that, you often look like you're a little clumsier than the other players," Murray says. "No, he was never a great skater. But he's worked at it. He still works at it today."

"EVERY DAY IS AN adjustment in the NHL — being prepared physically, being mentally ready for every practice and every game. But probably the biggest thing was just being there on my own." — Dany Heatley on his rookie season in the NHL

The youngster might not have taken to skating naturally, but he nevertheless jumped into hockey with everything he had. That's natural, since his father had been a junior forward with the Calgary Buffaloes in the mid-'60s before playing four years as a Badger forward at the University of Wisconsin.

After spending time with both Tulsa and Phoenix in the Toronto Maple Leafs' farm system, then three years in the World Hockey Association with the Minnesota Fighting Saints and the Indianapolis Racers, Murray Heatley headed to Germany, where he played a total of seven pro seasons. His career was highlighted by a 43-goal season with the Phoenix Roadrunners of the International Hockey League in 1972–73. So to his eldest son, a hockey career wasn't exactly a stretch of the imagination.

Still, Dany didn't show immediate signs of following in his father's footsteps. He loved playing road hockey with a tennis ball, which he did continually with his younger brother, but he was nine or 10 before he began to develop into one of the better minor hockey players in Calgary.

And it wasn't until his first year of midget, when he posted 30 goals and 42 assists in just 25 games and led the Calgary Blazers to the national Air Canada Cup championship — where he was named most valuable player — that Heatley began thinking about the game as a long-term proposition. "Probably in midget and junior I hoped to have a shot at it as a career," he recalls, "but I don't think it was a reality until I was probably in college."

BAUER
5
HEATLEY
CP95

Before he reached the Wisconsin campus, though, Heatley turned plenty of heads in the Alberta Junior Hockey League. In one amazing season as a 17-year-old with the Calgary Canucks, he posted 70 goals and 56 assists over 60 games to earn provincial and national junior A player-of-the-year honours.

That standout season, combined with his size and his puck pedigree, made Heatley a sought-after commodity among major junior and college scouts. But he never considered playing major junior hockey, mainly because of his father's terrific college experience.

Picking a college wasn't the easiest choice, however. He could have gone to any school that had a hockey program but Dany narrowed his choices to the total of five schools that he was allowed to visit under NCAA recruiting regulations. His first trip was to Ohio State. "Dany was blown away by Ohio State," recalls his father. "He came home and said, 'That's where I'm going.'"

Murray Heatley advised his son to make some other trips and take some time before making the crucial decision on where he would spend his college career. Wisconsin was his second visit and, after a weekend in Madison, the teenager's mind was made up. Heatley called his parents from the campus to announce his decision. He had found his school.

The choice proved to be a good one for Dany Heatley. Although he would not complete four years at the school, he turned in two outstanding seasons with the Badgers and absolutely loved the college lifestyle. In fact, he credits the experience at Wisconsin as the biggest reason he has adjusted so seamlessly to the NHL.

"I think college hockey is better hockey than major junior, just for the age factor," Heatley says. "You have to play against older guys, some as old as 24. In junior you can be playing against 16-year-olds and nobody's older than 21."

Heatley didn't seem to need much adjustment time once he joined the Badgers, however. As a freshman he made an immediate impact, playing on a line with future NHLer Stephen Reinprecht. Heatley finished his first college season with 28 goals and just as many assists in only 38 games. He was Western Collegiate Hockey Association rookie of the year and also cracked the league's first all-star team.

Heatley credits his time with the Badgers for helping him to improve his skating and his defensive play and enabling him to gain more than 20 pounds through strength training.

"You could see he was a big-time player. He had the size and the hands," recalls Red Berenson, the former NHL great and long-time University of Michigan coach. "He could just change the game with a couple of shifts."

Red Berenson wasn't the only one who noticed the big kid from Calgary. NHL scouts were all over Heatley as his freshman year of college coincided with his draft year. To make matters even more exciting, the NHL entry draft that June was to be held in his hometown of Calgary and Heatley spent a good portion of the season as the No. 1-ranked North American skater in the draft.

In a surprising turn of events, however, Dany Heatley didn't go No. 1 in the 2000 draft. New York Islanders general manager Mike Milbury had his sights set on Boston University freshman goaltender Rick DiPietro and Milbury engineered a dramatic trade to take DiPietro with the first pick overall, the highest selection ever used on a goaltender. Heatley instead went second overall to the Thrashers.

"We were all in the same boat," Heatley says of the top five players in the draft. "We were wondering whether we'd go one to five, there was so much talk. For me, it was not a matter of what pick I was, but where was I going to go. I was happy to go to Atlanta."

"Atlanta turned out to be a pretty good situation for him," adds Murray Heatley.

It certainly did. But before he joined the Thrashers, the 19-year-old decided to return for at least a second year at Wisconsin. "It was a huge decision to come back," Heatley says. "But it really helped me to prepare for the NHL — not just for hockey, but in terms of maturing and growing up."

The Badgers weren't complaining, either, as Heatley picked up where he left off as a freshman, scoring 24 goals and 58 points to crack the NCAA West First All-American team and become a finalist for the Hobey Baker Award, given annually to the national collegiate

A ROYAL VISIT

After he scored four goals in the first two periods of his first NHL All-Star Game, Dany Heatley received a surprise visit in the Eastern Conference dressing room. Hockey legend Wayne Gretzky sought out the youngster between periods and urged him to go for the All-Star goal record in the final frame, a record Gretzky then shared with three others. "It was very meaningful," Heatley told reporters later. "It was great to see him."

player of the year. By the end of that sophomore season he was ready to take the step up to the NHL, although few were aware just how ready.

Heatley barely missed a stride as he jumped into the big leagues as a 20-year-old. He played on a line with fellow rookie sensation Ilya Kovalchuk of Russia and the pair quickly became the biggest reason for Thrashers fans to watch their struggling team.

Heatley finished with 26 goals and 67 points playing the full 82-game regular season and averaging nearly 20 minutes per game of ice time. His totals were enough to land him a spot on the NHL All-Rookie team as well as the Calder Trophy, given to the league's rookie of the year, while Kovalchuk was the runner-up.

Heatley lived in an Atlanta-area apartment in his first NHL season. It was an adjustment, living on his own after being around plenty of college-age teammates for the previous two seasons. His family, including his mother and younger brother Mark, visited regularly and went to Atlanta for Christmas. And Dany spent a lot of time with Kovalchuk, his roommate on the road.

"Every day is an adjustment in the NHL — being prepared physically, being mentally ready for every practice and every game," Heatley says of that first season. "But probably the biggest thing was just being there on my own.

"I think for me the fact I was coming out of college is a big reason for my good start [in the NHL], though. In that second year at Wisconsin, I did a lot of growing up. I think that allowed me to deal with the NHL a lot better."

Heatley said he feels more and more comfortable in Atlanta each day as he grows accustomed to the NHL routine. He bought a house in Buckhead, a suburb of the Georgia city, before his second year with the Thrashers and he has slowly traded allegiances from his childhood baseball team, the Toronto Blue Jays, to the Atlanta Braves.

Far from experiencing a sophomore jinx, Heatley's second NHL season was even more impressive than his first. He was conscious not to try to overreach or set goals that were too onerous. "I just wanted to improve and work hard every day," he says. That approach paid off with 41 goals and 89 points, despite the fact that his Thrashers once again struggled, firing head coach Curt Fraser in midseason and replacing him with Bob Hartley. Playing on a different line than Kovalchuk, Heatley looked to score more often, beating his rookie goal total by 15 and firing 50 more shots on net.

Likely the most memorable part of the season for Heatley was his performance in the 53rd NHL All-Star Game. He scored four times in a 6-5 Eastern Conference loss, tying the All-Star record shared by Wayne Gretzky, Mike Gartner, Mario Lemieux and Vincent Damphousse. He also added an assist and scored a goal in the penalty shootout that decided the game. The latter didn't count in his official All-Star goal total but he was nevertheless the youngest player in All-Star history to record a hat trick.

Heatley was named the game's most valuable player and won a 2003 Dodge Ram pickup truck in his first appearance in the NHL midseason classic. With a BMW and a Porsche 911 already parked in his garage, the truck was forwarded to his little brother in Calgary.

The All-Star Game is certainly among his most memorable achievements in hockey to date. "It's definitely up there," Heatley says. "I was playing with two pretty good guys in that game [Jaromir Jagr and Olli Jokinen]. Those guys were giving me the puck and it was going in the net …"

Even more than his long reach, his uncanny ability to avoid hits and his deadly shot, his infectious smile is perhaps the most identifiable feature of the player teammates call "Heater." It's a unique smile because there is a large gap where he is missing a front, upper left tooth. During his first All-Star Game that smile, which seems to honestly relay in less than a second his passion for the game, became familiar to hockey fans across the world.

"He's probably one of the best hockey players in our game, and in my opinion he's a better person than he is a hockey player," Philadelphia forward Jeremy Roenick told reporters during All-Star weekend."He's polite, he's humble, he always wants to learn and he's always got a smile on his face."

Heatley's first two seasons in the NHL have left fans and contemporaries wondering just how good he can become. He says he feels more comfortable every day as he matures as an NHL player.

"I can definitely get stronger, quite a bit stronger," he says. "And I want to be mentally competitive every second out there."

Already he is seen by some as a leader of the next generation of NHL stars. In fact, in a recent *Sports Illustrated* poll of league general managers, Heatley was named as the young player they would most like to build a franchise around, ahead of even Boston's Joe Thornton. Murray Heatley believes his son will continue to improve "because he just lives and dies hockey."

As for his future aspirations, Heatley said he'd relish the chance to again play for Canada. He was part of two bronze-medal Canadian teams at the world junior tournament and he also suited up for his country during the 2002 and 2003 world championships. "Any time you get asked to play for your country it's an honour and I'd jump at the chance again," he says.

He'd also jump at any chance to help bring success to the Thrashers and their fans. He was made an assistant captain by Bob Hartley during his second NHL season and is widely seen as the long-term future captain of the Atlanta franchise.

"I just want to be part of this team growing up and bringing a Stanley Cup to Atlanta." HYS

BAUER
BAUER
ARMOUR FOAM
18

MARIAN HOSSA #18

OTTAWA SENATORS • RIGHT WING

Height: 6-1 Weight: 208 Born: January 12, 1979 — Stara Lubovna, Slovakia

Season	Team	GP	G	A	TP	PIM	+/-	Shots	Pct
1997–1998	Senators	7	0	1	1	0	-1	10	0.0
1998–1999	Senators	60	15	15	30	37	18	124	12.09
1999–2000	Senators	78	29	27	56	32	5	240	12.08
2000–2001	Senators	81	32	43	75	44	19	249	12.85
2001–2002	Senators	80	31	35	66	50	11	278	11.15
2002–2003	Senators	80	45	35	80	34	8	229	19.65
NHL Totals		386	152	156	308	197	60	1130	13.45

He was just 18 and a world away from his home in Slovakia. He was struggling with a new language, new food and a new way of life. And worst of all, he was being sent down.

Marian Hossa had just come clear across the world to play for the Ottawa Senators of the NHL. His plans had not included playing clear across the continent for the Portland Winterhawks of the Western Hockey League.

But after seven NHL regular-season games without a goal, the Senators were sending Hossa down to junior. The team had decided he needed some seasoning, both in a hockey and a cultural sense.

"I was disappointed when they sent me down," Hossa says now. "I didn't know if it was right or wrong."

Winterhawks general manager Ken Hodge recalls the Slovakian arriving in Portland during that first week of October 1997. The veteran junior hockey man sensed the talented teenager didn't understand why the Ottawa Senators weren't keeping him around.

"He had his heart set on being in Ottawa," Hodge recalls. "He was disappointed at being in Portland. But Ottawa wanted him to make the cultural adjustments he needed to make, on and off the ice."

Hossa didn't pout in the wake of the move. Quite the opposite, actually. He worked on his English, moving in with a billet family in Oregon's largest city, and he worked on his game, adjusting to the smaller ice surface and the more physical style of play in North America.

"There's a lot less ice in our game than he was used to in the European game, and not just because of the smaller size of the rink," Hodge says. "It took Marian some time to get used to people playing in his face. But the last half of the season, he was a dominant player in our league."

Hossa appeared in 53 games for Portland that year, finishing with 45 goals and 85 points. In the playoffs, he piled up 13 goals and 19 points in just 16 games as the Winterhawks captured both the WHL championship and the Memorial Cup. In the process, Hossa was named to the WHL, Canadian major junior and Memorial Cup all-star teams.

It wasn't an altogether glorious ending to Hossa's brief North American junior career, however. In the dying minutes of the Memorial Cup championship game against the Guelph Storm, he suffered a knee-on-knee collision with opponent Ryan Davis and had to be helped off the ice. With their star winger being attended to in the dressing room, the Winterhawks won the championship in overtime. Ken Hodge remembers pushing Hossa out onto the ice for the celebration and photographs afterward while the star was sitting in a chair. He couldn't even walk. "It was a bit of a sad and happy day for him," Hodge says.

While the championship was sweet, the news on the injury front was not. Hossa had suffered a torn left anterior cruciate ligament and would require surgery and extensive rehabilitation. He made a rapid recovery, returning to regular action by November, but the injury limited him to 60 games in his rookie NHL season with the Senators.

Despite the way it ended, Hossa looks back on the Portland experience as an important one in his hockey and personal development. "In the end, I had so much fun there," he says. "We won the cup, I learned English and I was able to speak with my teammates."

He also learned to enjoy the North American lifestyle. When he first arrived from Slovakia, he longed for the schnitzel and potato dinners his mother, Marika, had made for him back home. In North America, it seemed to Hossa, hockey players consumed an awful lot of pasta and lasagna. "I wasn't used to it," he says. "I was missing my Mom's cooking when I came here."

Hossa comes from a close and extremely interactive family. His father, Frank, is a former Czechoslovakian elite league star and current Slovakian national team coach. His younger brother, Marcel, followed in Marian's footsteps, playing in Portland for three seasons before joining the Montreal Canadiens' lineup full-time in 2002–3.

Marian remembers skating for the first time when he was about four years old, in his hometown of Trencin, a city of about 59,000 people near the borders of Poland, Austria and the Czech Republic. When his father's professional team had optional skates or free ice time, Frank Hossa would take Marian and Marcel onto the ice with him.

"Actually, I was not a great skater," Hossa admits with a laugh. "When I watch a tape of it, I see I was [awkward]."

Nevertheless, he was blessed with good hands. "I was always able to score goals," he says. "I could stickhandle. The skating wasn't as good as I wanted it to be."

Playing in the Slovakian minor system helped. In his country, minor teams would practise several times a week, increasing to five days a week before the players reached the age of 10. The only games or tournaments came on weekends. The emphasis was on skills rather than winning games and the poorer players were weeded out of the game as they grew older.

"Early on, we had no sticks or pucks on the ice, so we could learn how to skate properly," Hossa recalls. "Then they would give us sticks and have us skate around pylons with the puck."

The Hossa boys also played soccer, but both chose hockey when it was time for them to concentrate on one sport. For Marian, the choice was easy. "Soccer was fun, but I was better with my hands, so I chose hockey."

He slept, ate and breathed the game, playing three times a day, counting shinny and ball hockey. The lure then wasn't the hope of playing professionally, at least not until he was 16 or 17. It was simply the joy of the game. "When I was really young I never thought about playing hockey for a living," he says. "I loved it always. Hockey was all day for me."

Hossa quickly became one of the top players in Slovakia and, in fact, played for his father in a pair of world junior tournaments. While his father was certainly a hockey role model, the player Marian followed as a youngster was the same player followed by thousands of hockey-loving kids around the world.

"I really liked Wayne Gretzky," Hossa says. "He was a big hero in my hometown when I was growing up. I didn't have much chance to watch the NHL when I was young — just a couple of highlights on TV. But back then Gretzky was the No. 1 guy, so they showed him."

Hossa played just one season of junior in his homeland, racking up 42 goals and 91 points with Dukla-Trencin as a 16-year-old. The next season he joined the club's Slovakian elite league team, with which he put up 25 goals and 44 points playing against much older and more developed professionals.

That performance was enough to convince the Senators to take Hossa 12th overall in the 1997 NHL entry draft held in Pittsburgh. His entire immediate family was with him for

PUCK POPPA

NHLers Marian and Marcel Hossa didn't have to look far to find a hockey role model. Their father, Frank, played on the Czechoslovakian national team and later became an influential coach in Slovakian hockey. "He had lots of impact on my hockey and my brother's hockey," Marian says. "It is a little different playing for your father when he is the coach, but he treats you like other players and I played like he was a normal coach. After the game, though, he is your father."

the special day that represented the culmination of most hockey players' dreams. "I had no clue about the draft," Hossa recalls. "I wasn't expecting to go that high. But that day was something big, you know?"

The move to North America a few months later meant many adjustments. Hossa knew there were several Europeans in the Ottawa system, including Daniel Alfredsson, Radek Bonk and Alexei Yashin, something that made him feel more comfortable. But his English-language experience was limited to the few British-based classes he had taken during his school days in Slovakia.

"It was pretty difficult," he recalls now. "All of a sudden, the people were talking so fast and you have no idea what they're talking about. Everything was so different. Everything was just hard to learn."

"EARLY ON, WE HAD no sticks or pucks on the ice, so we could learn how to skate properly. Then they would give us sticks and have us skate around pylons with the puck."
—Marian Hossa on his earliest hockey days in Slovakia

It was the first time Hossa had been completely on his own, without any family around on a regular basis. "I was a little bit scared, but also a little bit excited. I mean, it was my No. 1 dream to play in the NHL."

Hossa made an instant impact when he arrived, playing well through training camp and the exhibition season for the Senators. But after recording just one assist in his first seven NHL games, he was sent to junior.

Ken Hodge recalls that despite the obvious disappointment Hossa felt, he still arrived in Portland with "the attitude of a very special athlete."

That meant a willingness to begin learning the defensive side of the game that would make him much more valuable to the Senators. Hossa admits now that he wasn't a particularly good defensive player when he arrived from Slovakia.

Hodge remembers that Hossa always practised, played and worked out with a giant smile on his face. He worked hard to learn English and he interacted well with Portland's loyal WHL fans. He set lofty goals and standards for himself and then set about reaching them. And although he realized that he possessed special talents, Hodge said, Hossa never set himself above others.

"I've seen a lot of very skilled players who don't come close to achieving what he has done," Hodge says.

That work ethic has carried on at the NHL level. Hossa's numbers have been on a steady rise since he tallied 15 goals and 30 points in 60 games of his rookie season, a year in which

BAUER
18

he was still recovering from knee surgery yet cracked the league's All-Rookie team.

His point totals grew to 56 and 75 in his second and third NHL seasons, respectively. He posted 31 goals and 66 points in his fourth NHL campaign, when he also played for Slovakia and recorded six points in just two games at the Salt Lake City Olympics.

But perhaps most impressive during his first four full NHL seasons was the fact that he never finished with a negative plus-minus rating. Not bad for a player who arrived in North America without much in the way of a defensive game.

It is not defence that Marian Hossa is known for, however. It is the points the six-foot-one, 200-pound left-winger puts up on the scoreboard and the offensive plays he routinely makes that have turned him into a fan favourite in Ottawa. He has used a combination of deft hands, strength, passing skill and hockey sense to become one of the up-and-coming offensive forces in the NHL.

In his fifth NHL season, his offensive output reached another level altogether as he contended for the league scoring lead, finishing with career bests of 45 goals, 35 assists and 80 points. His goal-scoring breakthrough reflected in his shooting percentage, which soared to a lofty 19.65 during that season.

Hossa has appeared in two NHL All-Star Games, in 2001 and 2003, the latter experience made even sweeter when brother Marcel was named to the Young Stars game in south Florida the same weekend.

"The difference is I'm older, a little more experienced," Hossa says of his 2002–3 season. "I'm learning just how to compete every night. I have more confidence."

That confidence came despite the Senators declaring bankruptcy early in the regular season. While Ottawa players missed one paycheque, Hossa and his mates weren't missing many opportunities as they streaked to the top of the NHL standings.

"The team is playing so well right now that it's easier for individuals to play well," Hossa said, about three-quarters of the way through the regular season. "There haven't really been any distractions [about the ownership situation]. Nobody cares about anything like that. We just come out and play hard."

Hossa kept that momentum going in the 2002–03 playoffs, racking up 16 points, including 11 assists, in 18 playoff games to help the Senators reach the Eastern Conference finals, where they lost in the seventh game to the New Jersey Devils.

Few play with more determination now than Marian Hossa. Ken Hodge says even he is surprised by the numbers his former star is putting up. Then again, considering Hossa's work ethic, Hodge says maybe he shouldn't be.

"We have had players more dominant as juniors than Marian, who didn't achieve as much as NHL players," says Hodge, who has been with the Winterhawks for 27 years.

"I am surprised at what he's doing. But then again, I'm not." 

JAROME IGINLA #12

CALGARY FLAMES • RIGHT WING

Height: 6-1 Weight: 207 Born: July 01, 1977 – Edmonton

Season	Team	GP	G	A	TP	PIM	+/-	Shots	Pct
1996–1997	Flames	82	21	29	50	37	-4	169	12.42
1997–1998	Flames	70	13	19	32	29	-10	154	8.44
1998–1999	Flames	82	28	23	51	58	1	211	13.27
1999–2000	Flames	77	29	34	63	26	0	256	11.32
2000–2001	Flames	77	31	40	71	62	-2	229	13.53
2001–2002	Flames	82	52	44	96	77	27	311	16.72
2002–2003	Flames	75	35	32	67	49	-10	316	11.07
NHL Totals		545	209	221	430	338	2	1646	12.69

It is difficult to imagine a single skater who's more important to his team than Jarome Iginla. When it comes to franchise players in the NHL, the rugged right-winger is the poster boy. But it wasn't all that long ago that Iginla felt like just another kid looking for ice time and wondering what he had to do to prove himself. In his first year of major junior, with the Kamloops Blazers of the WHL, Iginla found himself on the bench, or sometimes even in street clothes in the press box. When he did play, he was often limited to one shift per period. For a player who had scored 87 points in just 36 midget games as a bantam-age player the previous season, it was a rude awakening.

"That was very tough to take," Iginla says now. "It was a big adjustment."

It was the fall of 1993 and 16-year-old Jarome Iginla, a minor-hockey standout from the Edmonton suburb of St. Albert, was on his own in Kamloops, British Columbia. The Blazers owned his WHL rights and they were a powerhouse team. Rookies, even talented ones such as Iginla, were eased into the Kamloops organization.

"I was on a very good team," he recalls. "I felt I was as good as or better than some of the other young players in the league who were playing more on worse teams. It worked out in the long run, but it was difficult to take then."

Back home in St. Albert, Iginla's mother, Susan Schuchard, heard the frustration in her son's voice over the phone. He was playing only a minute in some games, he told her. The words of wisdom from home were golden. "If you only have a minute," she advised her frustrated son, "then make that minute count." Iginla obviously took that advice to heart. He continued to work diligently, getting quicker and stronger and forcing the coaching staff to give him more ice time as the Blazers steamed their way to the Memorial Cup national major junior championship. Iginla's totals for that season might now look unimpressive — six goals and 23 assists in 48 games — but he was just a 16-year-old playing in a tough circuit with players as old as 21.

While Iginla fretted at first about his progress, the Kamloops coaching staff certainly didn't worry. They knew they had a special talent and they were ecstatic about his work ethic. "The biggest thing I liked about Jarome is every practice he'd come and try to get better," recalls Don Hay, head coach with the Blazers at the time and later his coach with the Calgary Flames. "He really pushed himself."

Those who know him will tell you that Jarome Iginla has always pushed himself, always demanded more from within than anyone else would ask — ever since he first

"I'M LIVING MY DREAM. I feel really blessed and fortunate. I realize this is not going to last forever."
—Jarome Iginla

went roller skating with his mother as a five-year-old in St. Albert and promptly skated circles around her.

Jarome Arthur Leigh Adekunle Tig Junior Elvis Iginla — that's the official name on his birth certificate — was born on July 1, 1977, in Edmonton to the American-born Schuchard and her husband, Elvis Iginla, a university student who at 18 had emigrated from Lagos, Nigeria. The couple was divorced before Jarome was two and Susan received considerable help raising her son from her mom and dad in St. Albert, Richard and Frances Schuchard.

As a boy, Jarome played a number of sports — soccer, floor hockey, track and field, basketball, tennis, baseball and bowling. He also sang in music festivals, took part in speech arts competitions and played the recorder. One highlight his mom fondly recalls is Jarome singing "Where Is Love?" from the musical *Oliver!* in Edmonton's Kiwanis music festival.

Jarome was six when his aunt and her boyfriend took him to the neighbourhood rink for his first skate. "I fooled around on the ice for one day and I really enjoyed it," he says. "Then I got into hockey."

While Jarome kept in contact with his father, now an Edmonton lawyer, and enjoys a strong relationship with him to this day, his mother and grandparents raised him. They fully supported his involvement in hockey, making sure he had rides to the rink and that his skates were sharpened. And his grandparents, conveniently, lived just down the street from an outdoor rink.

At first, Jarome wanted to be a goalie and spent some time in net. But there wasn't enough action at that position and, by age nine, he was playing "out" full-time. At 10,

FLAMES
CCM
TACKS

when he made the St. Albert rep team, his interest in the game snowballed. "I always dreamed of playing in the NHL," Iginla says. "I never thought about the odds or chances of making it. That's just what I wanted to be."

Growing up in Edmonton, predictably he was a big fan of Oilers such as Wayne Gretzky and Mark Messier. But he was also significantly influenced by the presence of Grant Fuhr, the Oilers' outstanding goaltender and one of just a handful of black NHL players. Iginla says that Fuhr's presence on the Oilers made it easier for him to dream about the NHL. He even met Fuhr briefly at a baseball tournament when he was just 10.

"I heard other kids say things like: 'What are the odds?' [of a black player making the NHL]" Iginla says. "It was nice for me to be able to say that yeah, there is one. It was nice to know that it is possible."

Those who watched Jarome Iginla develop as a minor-hockey star in the Edmonton area had little doubt about his potential. His surname means "big tree" in his father's native language of Yoruba and by the time he reached bantam age the young Iginla was well on his way to the imposing six-foot-one, 207-pound frame he has today.

Don Hay, then the Kamloops Blazers' head coach, remembers seeing Iginla at an evaluation camp in Sherwood Park, Alberta. "We knew we had something special then," says Hay, now head coach of the American Hockey League's Utah Grizzlies.

Hay remembers Iginla as an exceedingly polite kid who was enthusiastic about being part of the team and did everything asked of him. "He was physically strong at that age, so he could compete. We had [future NHLer] Shane Doan with the Blazers at the time, too, which was good for Jarome. They were similar-style players. They kind of pushed each other."

Iginla remembers the move to Kamloops as a huge change. He was leaving family and friends and moving to a new city, and hockey was no longer just a game. He was now skating in front of crowds of 5,000 in Riverside Coliseum. "All of a sudden, we were practising every day," he says. "I had to get used to all the travel and still handling school. Sometimes we would get home from a trip at 7:30 in the morning and I had an 8:30 a.m. class. I just had time to run home, shower and go to school."

He might not have played as much as he wanted, but joining the Blazers as a 16-year-old allowed Iginla to ease into major junior before the pressure of his draft year. "He had his mind set on being an NHLer," says Ed Dempsey, an assistant coach with the Blazers when Iginla arrived and later the head coach during the star's final year with the team. "He had such a purpose to better himself. He was just like a sponge, so genuine, with so much energy."

By the time he reached his draft year, Iginla was playing a major role for the Blazers. As a 17-year-old he posted 33 goals and 38 assists to go along with 111 penalty minutes and helped Kamloops capture its second straight Memorial Cup title, where he won most-sportsmanlike-player honours.

That second season drew the attention of NHL scouts, making Iginla one of the top prospects for the entry draft that, coincidentally, was held in his hometown. The Dallas

Stars picked him 11th overall in that draft, creating a magical moment for Iginla's family in Edmonton.

As it turned out, Iginla wouldn't play a single game for the Stars. He returned to the Blazers for a third WHL season and, before that campaign was half-finished, his NHL rights were traded along with Corey Millen to Calgary in return for Joe Nieuwendyk.

Meanwhile, Iginla was putting up huge numbers for the Blazers. He finished his third WHL campaign with 63 goals, 136 points and 120 penalty minutes to make the Canadian major junior first all-star team. But the best was yet to come. In April 1996, Iginla was summoned to join the Calgary Flames for the playoffs. He scored his first NHL goal in his very first game against the Chicago Blackhawks. "One night you're just a huge hockey fan, reading every story in the newspaper about these guys and the next night you're playing against them," he says now.

Ironically, the two playoff games Iginla appeared in during that call-up were the last two that the Flames franchise has played. In Iginla's seven subsequent full NHL seasons, the club has missed the postseason every year.

Iginla posted an impressive 50 points, including 21 goals, in his first full season with the Flames to make the NHL All-Rookie team. While many point to the 2001–2 season as his breakthrough as an NHL superstar, he says the transformation actually began two seasons earlier, when he finished with 63 points, including 29 goals, in 77 games, and enjoyed a 16-game point streak.

The following season, his fifth in the NHL, Iginla was a training camp holdout before eventually signing a three-year deal three games into the regular season. Nevertheless, he managed to up his career-best total to 71 points in just 77 games. That set the stage for his best pro season to date, the 2001–2 campaign that established him as a major star.

Playing a full 82-game schedule, the Flames' right-winger exploded for 52 goals and 44 assists for 96 points, all easily career bests. Using his strength and skating ability to drive to the net and his soft hands and powerful shot to full effect, he was the only player in the NHL to score 50 times and won the Art Ross Trophy for capturing the league points title. He also took home the "Rocket" Richard Trophy for most goals and the Lester B. Pearson Award, given to the league's outstanding player as chosen by his peers. He was a first-team NHL All-Star, not to mention a key member of Canada's gold-medal-winning team at the 2002 Salt Lake City Olympics. Iginla earned four points in six Olympic games and he was instrumental in Canada's dramatic gold-medal win over the United States, scoring twice and adding an assist.

Iginla called the season "just another step" on a path that he has been trying to follow since he was a teenager. But he admits a surge of confidence was probably the difference that winter, along with the fact that he remained injury-free.

"I think there's an unbelievable amount of this game that is mental," he says. "There are so many skilled players in the league. The difference now is trying to make plays, risking things I might not have risked before. You know: do you just dump the puck in or do

BETTER LATE THAN NEVER

Scoring twice to lead Canada over the United States in the gold-medal game of the 2002 Salt Lake City Olympics is one of the proudest achievements of Jarome Iginla's career. But he was very nearly left off the squad by general manager Wayne Gretzky. Iginla was a late invitee to Team Canada training camp after Philadelphia forward Simon Gagne's availability was questionable due to a shoulder injury. Once he got the invitation Iginla made the most of it, playing so well that Gretzky had to keep him on.

you try to make that extra move?" Having the confidence to make that extra move, to take those risks without dwelling on mistakes is the key, he says.

That confidence came in handy during the 2002–3 season, which would test Iginla's resolve. He signed a two-year contract worth $13 million US just eight days before training camp opened to remain with the small-market Flames. But then Iginla and the Flames got off to a disappointingly slow start. Hampered by groin and hand injuries and plenty of attention from opposing checkers, he scored only six goals in the first 29 games. But when he was healthy he began putting up big numbers again, finishing the season strongly with 35 goals and 32 assists over 75 games, including 20 goals in 21 games during a late stretch.

Still, it was not the kind of season he or Flames fans had hoped for. Iginla's shooting percentage dropped from a career-best 16.72 percent to 11.07, and his plus-minus fell to minus-10 after a career-best plus-27 the season before. Worst of all, the Flames once again missed the playoffs.

"There's more pressure this year, for sure, with the big contract and leading the league in scoring last year," Iginla conceded as the season wound down. "But every year there's pressure. I put pressure on myself. We all put pressure on ourselves. Personally, I don't think that the expectations were too high. I wanted to have a better season than I did last year."

Iginla seems to embrace such pressure and accept that it goes with the territory. "He goes out there every night and wants to make sure he's the best player on the ice," says Colorado defenceman Derek Morris, a former teammate. "He wants to be the difference in every game and he usually is."

Iginla was relieved to see the NHL trade deadline pass in February 2003 after hearing rumours the Flames might dump his high salary. "I love playing here," he says. "I was given a great opportunity to play in a lot of key situations at a young age. We've missed the playoffs now for seven years and I'd like to be here when we turn the corner. I don't know if there's a better hockey city in the NHL for support."

There is probably not a better ambassador for the game than Iginla, either. Known as "Iggy" to his teammates, he is personable and friendly to a fault, so much so that the Flames' public relations staff must keep a strict watch so that he doesn't overextend himself with fans and media. As far as Iginla is concerned, giving back to the fans is the least he can do. "I'm living my dream," he says. "I feel really blessed and fortunate. I realize this is not going to last forever."

Following his breakthrough season, the attention focused on him grew to unprecedented heights, including a seven-page spread in *GQ* magazine. But no matter how big his celebrity, Iginla remains grounded. He and Kara Kirkland, whom he has known since junior high school, were married in the summer of 2003 and Jarome remains close with his family. "He's a really nice person," says his mom, "and that's what makes a mother proud."

Don Hay, his first junior coach, agrees. "He hasn't changed," Hay says. "He's still got that same smile on his face and he's very respectful." HYS

CCM
12

12

OLLI JOKINEN #12

FLORIDA PANTHERS • CENTRE

Height: 6-3 Weight: 205 Born: December 05, 1978 – Kuopio, Finland

Season	Team	GP	G	A	TP	PIM	+/-	Shots	Pct
1997–1998	Kings	8	0	0	0	6	-5	12	0.0
1998–1999	Kings	66	9	12	21	44	-10	87	10.34
1999–2000	Islanders	82	11	10	21	80	0	138	7.97
2000–2001	Panthers	78	6	10	16	106	-22	121	4.95
2001–2002	Panthers	80	9	20	29	98	-16	153	5.88
2002–2003	Panthers	81	36	29	65	79	-17	240	15.0
NHL Totals		395	71	81	152	413	-70	751	9.45

It was late fall of 2001 and Olli Jokinen had just about had enough. Not only had most of the NHL given up on his ever becoming a star, Jokinen was starting to wonder if the critics were right.

Through more than three full seasons in the NHL, the Finnish centre had shown nowhere near what had been expected of him when he was drafted third overall by the Los Angeles Kings in 1997. In the fall of 2001, he was already on his third NHL team, he wasn't producing points and his confidence level had sunk to an all-time low.

"I was thinking of going back to Finland," Jokinen admits. "I was playing on the fourth line and it was my fourth year in the league. I didn't want to be a fourth-liner."

Enter Mike Keenan, the head coach whom it seems NHL players either love or hate. Many might have predicted a disaster when the demanding Keenan met the underachieving Jokinen, but the opposite occurred. The arrival of "Iron Mike" in south Florida spurred the revival of Olli Jokinen as a star-calibre player. He finished that 2001–2 season playing as well as he had ever played in the NHL, and in the following season, his fifth full North American campaign, he blossomed into the player that scouts across the world had envisioned he could be when they first laid eyes on him.

Jokinen had scored a total of only 35 goals in parts of five seasons in North America prior to the 2002–3 campaign. But he finished with 36 goals in his fifth full season alone, adding 29 assists to become the surprise story of the NHL.

"I'm finally the player I wanted to be," Jokinen says, summing up that sweet breakout season.

After posting 41 points in 50 games as an 18-year-old playing for Helsinki IFK in the Finnish elite league, the six foot three, 205-pounder was considered one of the best, if not the best prospect in the world.

The Los Angeles Kings took him with the third pick overall in the 1997 draft and everybody, including Jokinen, had sky-high expectations. But those never materialized and the Kings gave up on him after only one full season, trading him to the New York Islanders. After a 1999–2000 season in Uniondale, New York, when he posted 21 points in 82 games, the Islanders also shipped him away, sending Jokinen and goaltender Roberto Luongo to Florida.

Things didn't go much better with the Panthers at first. Jokinen put up just 16 points in 78 games in his first season in Florida. And after another slow start in his fourth full NHL season, he was ready to call it quits in North America.

"I was close to signing with a Finnish club and going home," he says. "But I decided to wait until the [2001–02] season was over."

"IT WAS ALL ABOUT confidence in my game. I'm playing with a lot of confidence now." —Olli Jokinen

That proved to be a good decision for Olli Jokinen. Keenan replaced Duane Sutter as the Panthers' head coach on December 3 and Jokinen finished the season strongly, posting career highs of 20 assists and 29 points. He also played for Finland in the Salt Lake City Olympics, earning three points in four games. But the best was yet to come. He could feel it.

Jokinen trained hard all summer before the 2002–3 season and was optimistic heading into the first day of training camp. "I just had a feeling it was going to be a good year," he says.

Even Jokinen's wildest expectations couldn't have prepared him for the season he was about to have, however. When Keenan asked him during training camp what his statistical objectives were, Jokinen replied that he thought he could score 20 goals. Turns out, he had more in him. His previous high for goals in a season had been 11 in 1999–2000 with the Islanders. In 2002-3, he had 11 goals in the first month alone.

"Before the season, Keenan said, 'All those scouts in the world couldn't be wrong if they picked you third overall,'" Jokinen laughs.

The veteran coach orchestrated the transformation by giving his big centre more than 20 minutes of ice time a game, a spot on the first line and plenty of power-play time. He was also tough with his project when he had to be. Jokinen responded and began thriving under Keenan.

"I really liked the way he's coached," Jokinen says. "The best players — he's given those guys tons of ice time. And now I'm not sitting for every mistake."

Maybe the biggest thing Jokinen has received is a shot of confidence. He says he didn't have a clearly defined role in his early NHL years. Now he does. "When you're on the first line, the first power play and playing 25 minutes a night, that's your job," he says of his increased production. "You're expected to score."

Scoring was never a problem for Olli Jokinen growing up in Kuopio, a snowy city of about 86,000 people that is known as the centre of eastern Finland and is located 390 kilometres north of Helsinki. Jokinen started skating when he was three years old and by the time he started playing hockey at six he was far ahead of most other kids.

At first, he wanted to play goal, but the equipment was too expensive. And his father, Matti, a centre in the Finnish first division, managed to coax Olli to use his obvious skating skills to produce goals instead of stopping them.

"My dad played hockey and I basically grew up in hockey rinks," says Jokinen, who as a boy admired the gritty play of his countryman Esa Tikkanen of the Edmonton Oilers.

"Where I grew up, it's basically winter for eight months with rinks outside," he says. "I was able to skate every day. I was on the ice 12 hours a day."

Jokinen was also always among the smallest players on his teams during his early hockey years and often played with and against older players. He didn't experience a serious growth spurt until he was about 14. "When you're small, you have to learn to skate fast," he says.

By the time he was 16, he was already getting the idea he might be able to play hockey for a living and so he gave up soccer and volleyball to concentrate on his first sport. Russian Anatoli Bogdanov was coaching the elite league team in Kuopio. One day, he and young Jokinen had a conversation:

Bogdanov: "Do you want to go to school or do you want to be a hockey player?"

Jokinen: "I want to be a hockey player."

Bogdanov: "Welcome to the team."

That season, Jokinen played 15 games for the Kalpa Kuopio men's team. The next season he moved up to the club's elite league team and also played for Finland in the men's world championships. By then he was beginning to appear on every pro hockey scout's radar.

At 17, he left his hometown for Helsinki to sign with elite league powerhouse IFK. The move was a big one — he was now about five hours away from home by car — but the transition was eased by the presence of his brother Bille, two years older, who also signed with IFK. The two shared an apartment in Helsinki and a passion for hockey.

"It was a good chance for me," Jokinen says of the move. "It was my draft year and they said I would get a lot of ice time. It was difficult being a long way from home when you're 17, but that's what all the kids do in Canada if they want to play hockey."

Jokinen's 41-point output for IFK made him one of the top prospects in the 1997 NHL draft, held in Pittsburgh. His entire family attended. "It was a great experience," he recalls. "I didn't really know what to expect. I didn't know where I was going to go."

Los Angeles took Jokinen with the No. 3 pick, behind only top selection Joe Thornton and No. 2 Patrick Marleau, and one spot ahead of future teammate and current Panthers goalie Roberto Luongo. In going third overall he shared honours with Aki Berg, taken by Los Angeles in 1995, as the league's highest-ever-drafted Finn.

HE SHOOTS, HE ... Wonder why Olli Jokinen scored more goals in 2002–3 than in all of his previous four full NHL seasons combined? Well, it certainly helped that he took more shots — 87 more than his previous highest season, to be exact. Jokinen scored 36 times on 240 shots, compared with nine times on 153 shots in 2001-2.

Jokinen was still just 18 and his advisers told him to stay home one more year, do his mandatory service in the Finnish army and play hockey. But he wanted to get to the NHL as soon as possible.

The Kings brought him to Los Angeles and arranged for him to billet with an area family. He played eight games with the NHL club, failing to register a point, before returning to Finland for another season with IFK. Back home, he piled up 39 points in 30 games.

"I came back the next year to L.A. and I knew the routine," Jokinen says. "I went straight to live with the same family and I already had a car, a bank account, it was all set up."

What he wasn't ready for, however, was the culture shock or the language barrier. "It was different going to Los Angeles. It's a city of 15 million people and in Finland the whole country only has five million."

It was also different in the NHL, where the 82-game regular season was more than 30 games longer than any season he had played in Finland and where the players were bigger, stronger and much more physical. Although he fared well in the preseason, the regular season was another matter altogether. The ice surface was smaller than in Europe, there was more dumping and shooting and less holding onto the puck. Jokinen began to feel his confidence slowly slipping away. It was a slide that would continue until his revival in Florida.

"If I look back right now, I wasn't mentally ready to play in this league and physically I wasn't ready, either," he says.

Despite his slow start in Los Angeles he says the trade to the Islanders, which brought Ziggy Palffy to California, was a huge shock. He never felt comfortable in Long Island, playing with a team on which many of the players seemed to be just passing through. "It never felt like it was a home there," he says. "In my mind, I still wanted to be in L.A."

When he went back to Finland after his only season with the Islanders, Jokinen fully expected something to happen. "Basically the message was: If you're not in our plans for the first two lines, you're going to get traded," he recalls.

The trade came on June 20, 1999. Jokinen and Luongo were shipped to Florida in exchange for Mark Parrish and Oleg Kvasha. That trade would turn around the humble Finn's career.

"Sometimes it takes a little time and a little reassurance for them that they can play," Mike Keenan says, when asked what the difference in Jokinen has been.

Sometimes they just need the right coach, too, and the right situation. Jokinen has bloomed under Keenan, just as young, growing stars Joe Thornton, Jeremy Roenick and Chris Pronger did with the hard-nosed coach during earlier stops in his career.

"He challenges players every day," says Jokinen. "He tells you the truth. Sometimes it hurts, but you have to take it the right way."

While Keenan's style has been known to shake the confidence of some players, the effect has been just the opposite on Jokinen.

BAUER
12
A
UER
12
TRU FLEX

"It was all about confidence in my game," he admits. "I'm playing with a lot of confidence now. Once you start scoring, you expect to score every game. I'm mentally a lot stronger than I was before."

That mental strength hasn't been lost on observers. Florida general manager Rick Dudley told *USA Today* in 2002 that the change in Jokinen's approach to the game is that now "he skates every shift as if it is his last."

Perhaps another key to his revival on the ice is the fact that Jokinen and his wife Katarina are busy off the ice with daughter Alexandra, who turned three in the summer after her father's finest NHL season to date.

Jokinen says that when he came to the NHL as a teenager he thought about hockey 24 hours a day. Now, he puts the game into a little better perspective.

"She definitely keeps me busy," he says of his daughter. "That has helped me, too. I don't think hockey all the time."

Jokinen and his young family enjoy living in south Florida where the weather is nice and warm, especially for visiting relatives from Finland. The fans have warmed to him, too, giving the centre a standing ovation when he played in the 2003 NHL All-Star Game on the Panthers' home ice.

Jokinen replaced Saku Koivu of the Montreal Canadiens in the NHL classic, because Koivu was busy with medical tests connected to his recovery from cancer. But Jokinen was easily deserving of selection himself, with 25 goals at the All-Star break.

During the game he earned three assists and scored the goal that sent the contest into overtime while playing on a line with All-Star MVP Dany Heatley and superstar Jaromir Jagr.

"I never really dreamed about playing in the All-Star Game," he says. "I never thought that I was going to be part of that. It was a lot of fun, not just playing in the game but being around all those guys. It was a special moment. It was my first time. And playing at home, in front of the home crowd, it was amazing."

Jokinen was only 23 by the time he had completed his fifth NHL season. He can tell you from experience that players capable of stepping into the league as teenagers and putting up big numbers — such as Dany Heatley — are few and far between. Some, like Jokinen, need a little time to bloom.

"I still have a long way to go," he says, "to get to where I want to be." 

ILYA KOVALCHUK #17

ATLANTA THRASHERS • LEFT WING

Height: 6-2 Weight: 235 Born: April 15, 1983 – Tver, Russia

Season	Team	GP	G	A	TP	PIM	+/-	Shots	Pct
2001–2002	Thrashers	65	29	22	51	28	-19	184	15.76
2002–2003	Thrashers	81	38	29	67	57	-24	257	14.78
NHL Totals		146	67	51	118	85	-43	441	15.19

Of the multitude of words that have already been used to describe Ilya Kovalchuk during his brief NHL career, there is one on which everybody agrees: Scorer.

Whether he's capturing their hearts or getting under their skin, the NHL's newest Russian superstar has already shown everybody an ability to put the puck in the net that few young players have demonstrated at hockey's highest level.

As an 18-year-old, the flashy Kovalchuk scored 29 times in just 65 games for the Atlanta Thrashers. And had it not been for a dislocated shoulder that caused him to miss 17 games of the regular season, the rookie might well have wrested Calder Trophy honours from teammate Dany Heatley.

Kovalchuk's 29 goals were the most of any NHL rookie and his 51 points were second only to Heatley's 67 points while playing 17 more games.

"He's the most unbelievable scorer I've ever seen," Heatley says of Kovalchuk, his good friend on the Thrashers. "Watching him in practice scoring goals is ridiculous. He's got speed and a great shot. He's so exciting. He's got to be a fan favourite every time he touches the puck."

Unless, of course, you happen to be a fan in those NHL cities where Kovalchuk has rubbed crowds and opponents alike the wrong way with his flashy style and his tendency to showboat. Or unless you were part of the legion of fans cheering for the Canadian junior national team in 2001, when Kovalchuk pumped his fist in what many interpreted as a hot-dogging faux pas just before he scored the empty-net goal that clinched a victory over Canada and his future NHL teammate Heatley in the world championship semifinal.

This is the other side of Ilya Kovalchuk. The feisty, controversial side. While he brings pure scoring talent to the ice on every shift, he also brings pure attitude.

Kovalchuk possesses a swagger that sets him apart from many Russian or other European hockey players, a swagger that seems more akin to a major league baseball slugger or an NBA jam-master. He seems well aware of his special talents, a quality that grates

A SENSE OF HISTORY

Watching tapes of the 1972 Canada-Russia hockey Summit Series had a major influence on Ilya Kovalchuk's career path, though he was born 11 years after the epic eight-game showdown was played. In fact, Kovalchuk now wears No. 17 with the Atlanta Thrashers in honour of the late Valeri Kharlamov, a great Soviet star of 1972.

some who play, and cheer, against him. That confidence is just fine with his own NHL organization, however.

"He believes that he'll be the best player in the world," says Thrashers general manager Don Waddell, the man most responsible for drafting Kovalchuk to the Deep South. "And I don't mind that one bit."

That swagger also serves to make Kovalchuk endlessly entertaining. Despite a language barrier that still requires a translator for more in-depth interviews, the left-winger already surprises with a depth of perception lacking in the warmed-over observations of far too many professional athletes.

When asked about the difficulty of being thrown into the NHL without any command of English, for instance, he describes the experience in this insightful manner: "I was like dog. People could speak to me, but I could not speak to them."

Ilya Kovalchuk has always been able to speak with his hockey stick, or at least since his father, Valeri, began taking the four-year-old to the rink in their hometown of Tver, a central Russian city of about 460,000 on the Volga River, just a short drive from Moscow.

Valeri Kovalchuk was not a hockey player himself. He played basketball for a Russian first-division professional team and later worked at a boarding school and ran a sporting-goods shop. But he enrolled his only son in hockey school in Tver and showed young Ilya videos of the historic 1972 Summit Series, in which Canada squeaked out a victory over the Soviet Union in eight games.

That series opened the door for regular competition between the best hockey players from two different global factions and, ultimately, for the internationalization of the NHL. Watching grainy video of the Summit Series also played a huge role in Ilya Kovalchuk's love for the sport.

From his earliest days on the ice, Kovalchuk showed a natural talent for finding the net. "I was always the best goal-scorer," he says of his early days playing the game. "I don't know why. I shoot the puck."

That obvious talent led to a quick rise through the Russian hockey system, during which he developed his confidence by playing ahead of his age group. By the time he was 16 he was already playing for Spartak Moscow in the Russian professional league. As a 17-year-old he dominated the Russian league, scoring 42 goals and adding 22 assists in 65 games. His scoring touch helped Spartak top the Russian first division that season, lifting the club into the Superligue for the following winter.

Kovalchuk also put in some sterling performances for Russia as a teenager on the international stage. In the world under-17 tournament at Timmins, Ontario, for example, he piled up 14 points, including 10 goals, in just a half dozen games. After that performance, the Hockey Hall of Fame in Toronto requested one of the young Russian's sticks for its collection.

Don Waddell first saw his future Thrasher star at the 2000 Four Nations tournament in Salt Lake City, when Kovalchuk was only 16. During that competition he scored four goals

EASTON

and added three assists over four games to power Russia to the championship.

"There's no doubt that the first time I saw him, I knew he was a take-charge guy. He wanted to have the puck on his stick all the time ... He's a guy you notice on the ice.

Atlanta scouts weren't alone in coveting Kovalchuk in the lead-up to the 2001 NHL draft in Sunrise, Florida. Kovalchuk was ranked No. 1 by NHL Central Scouting both at midseason and at the end of the year. The Russian had a fiery aggression to his game that reminded scouts of Rocket Richard and the size — at six foot two and 207 pounds — to back up that edge. When the Thrashers won the draft lottery and the right to pick first overall, there was absolutely no doubt whose name Waddell would call. Kovalchuk had impressed enough to become the first Russian to be drafted No. 1 overall in the history of the NHL, above

"I WAS LIKE DOG. People could speak to me, but I could not speak to them."
— Ilya Kovalchuk, on learning English as a rookie in the NHL

previous stars such as Pavel Bure, Igor Larionov, Alexander Mogilny and Sergei Fedorov. The highest earlier Russian draftee was Alexei Yashin, who went No. 2 to the Ottawa Senators in 1992.

The Thrashers were certainly aware of Kovalchuk's well-documented confidence when they drafted, but they weren't worried about him being hard to handle. Waddell believes it is always easier to take the cockiness out of a player than to try to instill the type of drive — or duplicate the level of talent — this Russian teen obviously possessed.

In pre-draft interviews they discovered an intelligent young man who savours scoring, but also enjoys classic Russian literature by the likes of Alexander Puskin. They discovered a remarkable athletic talent who comes from an academically inclined family. His mother, Zula, is a dentist and his sister, Arina, seven years his senior, is a lawyer.

"We knew all along that we would pick him," Waddell recalls. "We thought he was the best guy in the draft. We knew that he was going to be a special player."

The Thrashers retained the right to draft Kovalchuk even though they received plenty of offers from other teams. The honour of being No. 1 overall, ahead even of Canadian junior phenom Jason Spezza, was important to Kovalchuk, who displays a burning desire to prove his abilities every time he hits the ice. And that desire certainly didn't diminish once he hit North America.

He combined on a line with fellow rookie and teen sensation Dany Heatley to put up eye-opening numbers during the 2001–2 NHL season. He also played for Russia in the 2002 Salt Lake City Olympic tournament, scoring a goal and two assists to help his country to the bronze medal.

The season was highlighted by Kovalchuk's other worldly performance during February's

NHL All-Star Weekend at the Staples Center in Los Angeles, when he scored six times in a 13-7 Eastern Conference victory over the West in the Young Guns game. For any hockey fans who hadn't yet noticed, the showcase dramatically announced the Russian rookie's arrival in the NHL.

After the game, an interpreter attempted to relay Kovalchuk's approach to the event to journalists who asked: Had the Russian taken it seriously? Had he been trying to prove something?

"He just showed what he wanted to," the interpreter said. "He can't say that he took it very seriously. He just showed everything he could."

Kovalchuk's impressive first-year numbers were enough to land him NHL All-Rookie honours. They came despite his missing nearly a fifth of the season to injury and despite having to adapt on the fly to a new culture and language.

He began rooming with Heatley at a Thrashers rookie camp in Michigan and that arrangement continued through their first season. The two quickly became good friends in spite of the fact that they would also go neck-and-neck in the Calder race, marking the first time teammates had finished one-two in the rookie voting since Brian Leetch and Tony Granato of the Rangers did so in 1989.

The friendship helped Kovalchuk learn English, but it was still slow going. It wasn't until late in his rookie season that he became comfortable enough even to order room service in their hotel.

Kovalchuk returned to Russia in the off-season and worked to make himself physically stronger and his shot even better. When he returned for his second season he picked up right where he left off, scoring 38 goals and adding 29 assists in 81 games. Helping him to feel more at home was the fact that his parents were able to spend much of the season in Atlanta.

That sophomore season included a well-documented fight with Edmonton Oilers' sniper and fellow NHL Young Gun Mike Comrie in December. The scrap drew chuckles from sportscasters across North America as it seemed to pit two of the league's most unlikely combatants, a couple of players known much more for their magic with the puck than with their fists. Still, truth be known, Kovalchuk is hardly averse to fighting. He dropped the gloves regularly in Russian hockey, piling up a conspicuous 112 penalty minutes during his final season at home. "I enjoy the physical part of the game," he says now. "If somebody gets into my kitchen, I can take care of myself."

That sort of candid reply will no doubt make Kovalchuk a media favourite in NHL cities, particularly as his English improves with each year spent in North America. When asked if he feels capable of 50-goal seasons and winning league scoring titles, he is refreshingly candid. "Very soon, hopefully," he replies. Asked whether he can become Russia's greatest NHLer, he says without hesitation, "Time will tell."

"I simply do not know what fear is while being on the ice," Kovalchuk once told *Red Line Report,* an independent newsletter aimed at NHL scouts. "Hockey should be played only by

real men, shouldn't it? If you want to be safe, then do not step onto the ice. If you play this game, then be ready to fight!"

Kovalchuk's scoring ability comes from a combination of speed, size, puck-handling skills, creativity and competitiveness. With his thick, powerful frame, he is able to put a lot of authority behind his shot, which he works on constantly, firing on net between 70 and 80 times every practice.

Waddell believes a big part of the reason Kovalchuk is a natural scorer is that he always wants the puck on his stick. "I've watched him, literally, take the puck off his teammates' sticks," Waddell chuckles.

When asked what makes a good scorer, Kovalchuk provides a thoughtful answer. "It should be everything," he told an NHL.com chat. "The goal scorer should be complete player, and he cannot have only speed or only shot to be a goal scorer. He has to have everything in combo."

The Thrashers would like Kovalchuk to add a little more defensive responsibility to that combo. While he possesses the kind of moves and scoring talent that can literally lift fans out of their seats, he still has plenty of work to do learning the other end of the game.

His point totals might have been noteworthy during his first two NHL seasons but so were his plus-minus totals. He was a dreadful minus-19 over his rookie season and slipped even further in Year 2 with a minus-24 rating. Waddell says Kovalchuk has made strides on the defensive end but, on more than one occasion during his second season, the Russian was benched by the Thrashers for lacklustre defensive effort.

“That was the only way to get his attention, to take away his ice time,” Waddell says. “He’s never going to win the Selke Trophy [for the NHL’s top defensive forward]. We know he’s not going to be a great defensive player. All we want is for him to be somebody who is reliable [defensively].”

Kovalchuk’s attitude has also been questioned by some opponents and members of the hockey media who see him as a show-off without sufficient respect for the opposition or even the game itself. During his second season with the Thrashers, one NHL columnist referred to Kovalchuk as “19 going on 15.”

The brash Atlanta star drew the wrath of the hometown Edmonton Oilers in February of his rookie season. After serving a two-minute penalty for using an illegal stick, Kovalchuk jumped onto the ice to grab a pass and scored on the resulting breakaway. Seconds later, he skated past the Oilers’ bench and asked, “Is this stick okay?”

While he has been widely criticized for that and other actions since he came to the NHL, Kovalchuk is described by Waddell as “a great kid off the ice,” a player whom he has never seen turn down an autograph request from a youngster.

“His cockiness is to be the best player he can possibly be and to help his team win games,” says the Thrashers’ general manager. “It’s not to show up other players or disrespect the game. I think if there’s one thing that our sport desperately needs, [it’s] some colour.”

Not to mention scoring. Waddell sees in Kovalchuk similarities to Peter Forsberg and Pavel Bure. The veteran hockey man sees a player with speed, passion, the capability of making dynamic moves with the puck, and no fear of either taking a hit or giving one.

“I think he’s a potential 50-goal scorer in the NHL,” Waddell says. “That’s something very few players in the league are capable of these days.” HYS

JOFA
4
A
Tampa Bay
LIGHTNING
THWES
RLINES
CCM

VINCENT LECAVALIER #4

TAMPA BAY LIGHTNING • CENTRE

Height: 6-4 Weight: 207 Born: April 21, 1980 – Ile Bizard, PQ

Season	Team	GP	G	A	TP	PIM	+/-	Shots	Pct
1998–1999	Lightning	82	13	15	28	23	-19	125	10.4
1999–2000	Lightning	80	25	42	67	43	-25	166	15.06
2000–2001	Lightning	68	23	28	51	66	-26	165	13.93
2001–2002	Lightning	76	20	17	37	61	-18	164	12.19
2002–2003	Lightning	80	33	45	78	39	0	274	12.04
NHL Totals		386	114	147	261	232	-88	894	12.75

It's difficult enough to break into the NHL as a slender youngster of 18, facing hardened veterans as much as 10 or 15 years older and 40 to 50 pounds heavier. But that task is even more daunting when you're saddled with impossible expectations such as, say, being labelled "the Michael Jordan of hockey." Such was the case in September 1998 for teenage phenom Vincent Lecavalier when he arrived in Florida as the supposed saviour of the terrible Tampa Bay Lightning and was hailed as M.J. on ice by overenthusiastic team owner Art Williams.

Lecavalier went to the Lightning as the consensus No. 1 overall draft pick, a French-Canadian junior hockey can't-miss kid with the good looks, smooth moves and long reach of a Jean Beliveau reincarnate. Perhaps predictably, however, it has taken a few seasons and some less than sunny times in Florida for Lecavalier to hit his stride with the 'Bolts. That finally happened during the 2002–3 NHL season, when the rangy centre posted career-best totals of 33 goals and 45 assists while leading the Lightning to the Southeast Division title and only their second-ever playoff spot.

"I just think I'm more consistent now," Lecavalier says, trying to explain by far his best NHL season to date. "I think as you get older you're more focused, you're more ready every game.

"At 18, you're still in junior mode. You might have two good games, then one bad game. In the NHL, you've got to be ready every single night. And it's tough to produce in the NHL every night."

Vincent Lecavalier has seldom had trouble producing offence since he began skating at age 2 1/2 when his father, Yvon, a former junior player himself, took his youngest boy to the rink in Pierrefonds near the family's hometown in Ile Bizard, Quebec, a suburb of Montreal.

"Obviously, at 2 1/2 you're going to fall a few times," Lecavalier says with a laugh.

That early start led to the youngster playing in his first organized hockey league at age four, skating alongside six- and seven-year-olds. By the time he was six, he was playing with and against nine- and 10-year-olds.

"I think that does help to play against older players, especially when you're young," Lecavalier says. "And I think I was ahead just by having skated at 2 1/2."

When he reached the atom level he reverted to playing with his own age group. He was still small in stature and many of the older boys had already grown much bigger. But in his first bantam season he sprouted six inches, putting him well on the way to reaching his adult height of six foot four.

"IN THE NHL, you've got to be ready every single night. And it's tough to produce in the NHL every night." — Vincent Lecavalier

Growing up, Vincent enjoyed soccer, baseball and golf. But at age 14 it was time to get serious about hockey and Lecavalier and his family made the difficult decision that he would leave home to pursue the game. He moved halfway across the country to the tiny south Saskatchewan town of Wilcox, population 200, a farming community that is also home to Athol Murray College of Notre Dame. The non-sectarian boarding school run by the Roman Catholic Church has nearly 400 students and a vaunted hockey program that has produced a number of NHL players including Wendel Clark, Russ Courtnall, Rod Brindamour and Gary Leeman. But Lecavalier attended the school chiefly because his older brother, Phil, had gone there and as a result had earned a U.S. college scholarship to Clarkson University in Potsdam, New York. That was the master plan for Vincent, too. He knew that going to Notre Dame would help his hockey career, but leaving home at 14 was difficult. "I was pretty homesick when I left," he recalls.

Things got better once the hockey season started in October, and once he made some friends at Notre Dame. Included among those school buddies was Brad Richards, a much smaller, more intense boy from Prince Edward Island. The two were the only grade 9 students at the college to make the Hounds bantam lineup and they quickly developed a bond that lasts until this day, as Lecavalier and Richards went on to become teammates in both junior hockey and the NHL.

"We've always been best friends," Lecavalier says of Richards, with whom he rooms on the road with the Lightning and lives beside in a Tampa condo development.

Terry O'Malley, who has worked and coached at Notre Dame for more than 25 years, remembers the two youngsters being inseparable, rooming together at the boarding school, playing ball hockey and hanging out. "They did everything together," O'Malley says. "They competed with each other, in an encouraging way. I think they both have a real joy for the game."

O'Malley remembers Lecavalier as a lanky young fellow who was extremely polite and coachable. He could tell the tall kid came from a good family. "If I could think of a gentleman, I'd think of him."

Lecavalier was also undeniably talented. He had a long, fluid skating stride and an ability to do impressive things with the puck for a player his size.

"For a fellow that age, he had tremendous coordination," O'Malley recalls. "You could see he was going to be a dandy hockey player."

At Notre Dame the students played hockey every day and Lecavalier adapted a more disciplined approach to the game, emulating his hockey heroes such as Steve Yzerman, Mario Lemieux and, yes, even Jean Beliveau, whose No. 4 he wore while with the Hounds and still carries to this day as a member of the Lightning.

Lecavalier was the Notre Dame bantam team's second-line centre in his first year at the college. But in his second season with the Hounds, as a 15-year-old, he exploded for 52 goals and 52 assists in just 22 bantam games. He was subsequently called up as an underage by the school's midget team for the playoffs and proceeded to lead the squad in postseason scoring.

Those accomplishments attracted plenty of interest from junior scouts in his home province, but Lecavalier had his sights set on going the scholarship route — that is, he did until he was drafted by the Quebec Major Junior Hockey League franchise in Rimouski, a six-hour drive from his hometown.

The Rimouski Oceanic offered a nice setting of about 50,000 people in the picturesque St. Lawrence River Valley, and a chance for Lecavalier to play in his home province while at the same time placing a heavy emphasis on his education. It was an enticing enough package to make the youngster opt for major junior hockey instead of the college path taken by his older brother. "If any other junior team was going to draft me, I was going to college," he says.

Instead, Lecavalier took most of his QMJHL opponents to school in just two seasons as a junior superstar. As a 16-year-old, he posted 42 goals and 61 assists to earn Quebec and Canadian major junior rookie-of-the-year honours. "That's when I probably realized that maybe I had a chance to play hockey for a living," he says now. "Before that, I didn't have a clue."

In his draft year, playing on an Oceanic team that included Brad Richards, Lecavalier piled up 115 points, including 71 assists, while amassing 117 penalty minutes — all in just 58 games. He also took English lessons and hired a personal trainer to prepare himself for his next step up the hockey ladder, to the NHL.

Those notable numbers — combined with his size and his silky skating stride — made Lecavalier the easy No. 1 choice of the Tampa Bay Lightning during the 1998 NHL entry

A MODEL PLAYER

Vincent Lecavalier's talents are not limited to the ice. He has also appeared as a model in a few major magazine fashion spreads, including the 2003 SPORTS ILLUSTRATED Swimsuit Edition. In that publication, he posed shirtless with girlfriend and model Caroline Portelance sitting on his knee, partially covered in a Lightning sweater. Lecavalier has also appeared on the pages of VANITY FAIR and GQ magazines.

draft held in Buffalo. Fifty of his friends and relatives made the trip south from Quebec for the event, during which both he and his longtime friend, Richards, who went 64th overall, were drafted by the Lightning. "It was pretty special," Vincent recalls. "I wanted to go first overall. But when you get drafted, it doesn't mean you're going to the NHL."

Somebody should have informed then Lightning owner Art Williams that hockey players sometimes take a little longer to develop than basketball blue-chippers. After selecting the Quebec junior star, Williams proclaimed Lecavalier "the Michael Jordan of hockey," a boast that would come back to haunt the owner and the struggling franchise, if not Lecavalier himself.

"I just think he was really excited about purchasing the team and it was his first year," Lecavalier says , forgivingly. "Obviously, I was 18. I wasn't assured of even making the team [that first year]."

Head coach Jacques Demers opted to keep Lecavalier with the NHL club from the start, rather than send him back to junior. But he was subsequently criticized for not giving Lecavalier enough ice time, as the rookie averaged less than 14 minutes per game. Wrote Tom Jones of the St. Petersburg *Times* early that rookie season, "Michael Jordan plays more than 11 minutes a game. Or, to put it another way, it's hard to save a franchise when you're on the ice less than the Zamboni."

Lecavalier finished that rookie season with respectable, if unspectacular, totals of 13 goals and 15 assists over a full 82-game schedule.

"I think the biggest difference was the strength of the defencemen in their zone," Lecavalier recalls of his initial adjustment to the NHL. "Guys were just stronger. They were 30, 40 or 50 pounds heavier than junior players. They just pushed me around in the corners."

Lecavalier made major strides as a 19-year-old, putting up 25 goals and 42 assists over 80 games during his second NHL season. In his third campaign, he managed 51 points in 68 games and was named team captain at age 20. Expectations for "Kid Lightning" remained sky-high. But prior to his fourth NHL season, Lecavalier was a training-camp holdout. He missed a month of preparation and was distracted by a rift with head coach John Tortorella over playing time and how he was being utilized. That led to his being dumped as team captain and heavy trade speculation. The cumulative result was a dismal 37-point campaign — with just 17 assists — in his fourth NHL season and nagging doubt about his future as the saviour of the Tampa Bay Lightning.

"That year, with only 37 points, was pretty tough," he recalls. "There were a lot of distractions and a lot of trade rumours. It was a tough year, but it's how you get back up [that counts]."

Lecavalier responded by undertaking a rigorous training routine over the summer of 2002. He reported to training camp that fall in the best shape of his career, setting the stage for his finest season yet as an NHLer. Not only did he have a breakthrough year offensively

JOFA
Tampa Bay
LIGHTNING
A
4
CCM
LECAVALIER
Tampa Bay
LIGHTNING
JOFA

with 78 points, he also managed an even plus-minus rating, by far the best of his NHL career; prior to 2002–3 he had never finished a season with better than a minus-18 rating. His 274 shots were more than 100 over any of his previous seasons. In his first career playoff appearance, Lecavalier finished with three goals and six points in 11 games as Tampa Bay reached the second round.

The Lightning forward credits his improved production to the general talent level of his Tampa Bay teammates, particularly his linemate, Czech Republic native Vaclav Prospal. "Prospal is such a great passer," Lecavalier says. "He gives me so many opportunities to score."

Brad Richards says the success of his best buddy and teammate was indicative of what the team did during that season, the finest to date for the Lightning franchise. "He stepped up his play this year," Richards says. "When he's on his game and he dominates with his speed and reach, he can do a lot of damage. It's fun to watch him." There is even a "mean" component to his game, says Richards, who describes Lecavalier as a mix between Joe Thornton and Mike Modano.

Lecavalier believes he can improve and will do so during the coming seasons. He is still young, after all, though already a five-year NHL veteran at age 23.

"I hope I'm not at the point where I can't get better," he says. "I think players peak somewhere between about 28 and 33. I want to get better every year. I think that's my goal."

Though he learned the game in Quebec and dreamed as a youngster about playing in Montreal, Lecavalier enjoys life in Tampa Bay. He was the focal point of the team's advertising campaigns as a rookie and has developed a following in the city and amongst hockey fans in the U.S. In 2002, he was voted hottest single NHL player on the ice by the match.com website, gaining 32 per cent of the vote.

"I can only imagine what it would be like playing in Montreal," he says. "But I like Tampa. Everything's good. The organization's great. When the team is winning, the support is there. They're good hockey fans. It's a great city and it's warm."

As for the way his NHL career has evolved, Lecavalier says if he had to do it all again he would still come to the NHL as a heralded 18-year-old. There was pressure, yes, but there was also opportunity.

"I think it was a great move," he says. "At 18, maybe you're not ready physically or mentally, but you learn very quickly." HYS

ROBERTO LUONGO #1

FLORIDA PANTHERS • GOALIE

Height: 6-3 Weight: 205 Born: April 04, 1979 – Montreal

Season	Team	GMS	MIN	W	L	T	GA	SO	Avg
1999–2000	Islanders	24	1292	7	14	1	70	1	3.25
2000–2001	Panthers	47	2628	12	24	7	107	5	2.44
2001–2002	Panthers	58	3030	16	33	4	140	4	2.77
2002–2003	Panthers	65	3627	20	34	7	164	6	2.71
NHL Totals		194	10577	55	105	19	481	16	2.73

The "best young goalie in hockey" is a label that has been attached to Roberto Luongo for a long time. Too long, if you ask the Florida Panthers' prime puck stopper himself.

"I think I'm past that point now," the articulate native of St. Leonard, Quebec, says in a midseason interview during his most recent NHL campaign. "I mean, I'm 23 years old. This is my fourth year in the league. Best young goalie? I'd like to be referred to right now as simply one of the best in the league."

Mission accomplished. Luongo has moved past the stage of prime prospect and earned the respect of players and coaches around the league as a goalie who is capable of stealing games. His success is coming with the young Panthers after a disappointing start to his career with the New York Islanders that ended with a trade to Florida on June 24, 2000.

The Islanders moved out Luongo, along with young centre Olli Jokinen, in exchange for forwards Mark Parrish and Oleg Kvasha. The trade has turned out to be magic for both Jokinen and Luongo, who have hit their strides as pros, as well as for the Panthers as a team.

A sinewy six foot three with wavy black hair and a dark complexion, Luongo has started to live up to the expectations brought on by a standout junior career in the Quebec Major Junior Hockey League and a silver-medal turn for Canada at the 1999 world junior championships.

It was after that tournament that Luongo was tagged with the "best young goalie" description. Such labels can be a curse, however, because potential is often a difficult thing to live up to, particularly as a young goaltender trying to learn his trade on the fly in the unforgiving NHL.

But Luongo has managed to do just that, becoming the No. 1 netminding option for the Panthers. And he credits time, rather than the change of scenery, as the biggest reason he has come of age in the NHL.

"I'm gaining experience," he says. "So the more I play, the more I feel comfortable."

Although he split time with Jani Hurme during the 2002–3 season as head coach Mike Keenan tried to ride his hottest netminder, the 24-year-old Luongo is considered the goaltender of the present and future in south Florida.

"His legs are almost illegal, they're so long," former Panthers assistant coach Paul Baxter says of Luongo. "He gets across the net better than any goalie in the league. You think you've got him beat and all of a sudden he's got his foot against the post and you don't know how he got from the other side."

Watch Luongo shoot rapidly across the crease to stop a sure goal, or rocket out his glove hand to snap a puck ticketed for the top corner, and it seems as though he was born to play goal. But he wasn't. In fact, he was a skater for his first three years of minor hockey in Montreal because goaltending equipment was too expensive.

When he finally went between the pipes, Luongo patterned himself after Edmonton

"[LUONGO] HAS tremendous attention to detail, which is vital for a goaltender in today's game ... There's never a day where he is not addressing the fundamentals of his game. I think every great goalie does that." — Former Panthers goaltending coach Ian Clark

Oilers great Grant Fuhr, whose quick reflexes and penchant for big glove saves were more intriguing characteristics to Roberto than the butterfly style of Patrick Roy or another of the Quebec-raised goalies one might expect a kid from Montreal to idolize.

"Roy was the guy we saw on TV, obviously, every night in Montreal and I really have a lot of admiration for Patrick," Luongo says. "But Grant Fuhr and his glove saves are really what attracted me first to being a goaltender. Grant Fuhr was my idol growing up."

It's interesting, then, that Panthers coach Mike Keenan, who has a well-earned reputation for playing mind games with his goalies, compares his young Florida lineup to that of the early Oilers. For his part, Luongo certainly doesn't mind being the Panthers' Grant Fuhr. And he doesn't seem to mind playing for Keenan, who earlier in his career earned the nickname "Captain Hook" for his lack of patience with struggling netminders.

"He obviously demands the most of not only his goaltenders but everybody on the ice, so you've got to be aware of that and just be ready to play every night," Luongo says. "As long as you do that, you won't have any problems."

Luongo, with his tiger-striped goalie pads and his sheer size and quickness in net, more often than not is the one posing problems — for opposing shooters. Since he came into the league he has worked hard to improve his positioning, helping him to become more consistent. If pucks are hitting him square in the chest, he says, he is in the right spot. In his fourth NHL season with the Panthers, he was often in the right spot.

"Technically, Roberto's very sound," Baxter says. "He's very skilled. He understands the

THE WORLD WAS WATCHING

Roberto Luongo made a name for himself in the sport internationally during the 1999 world junior championships in Winnipeg, where he was named the tournament's top goaltender despite Canada's 3-2 overtime loss to Russia — a championship game in which he faced 40 shots. During that tournament he posted two shutouts in seven games and a sparkling .940 save percentage, cementing his reputation as a big-game, big-save netminder with almost unlimited pro potential.

game. He's a calm, level-headed guy. He doesn't get too high, doesn't get too low ... He's going to be an exceptional goaltender for a long time."

Goaltending coach Ian Clark, who worked for the Panthers during the 2001–2 season, says the combination of Luongo's size, athleticism, agility and technical proficiency make him one of the best in the game already. "When you combine those elements, you've got a pretty good goalie."

Clark sees some validity in comparisons to Fuhr. "Grant Fuhr was a competitor," he says. "That's one of the things that Roberto is. He has an incredible knack for making saves at key times. He's one of the best goalkeepers in the game, down low when there's a scramble, for just somehow finding a way to stop pucks. Grant was also a guy who found ways to stop pucks, so there's a parallel."

Now a coach with the Vancouver Canucks, Clark says Luongo is extremely detail-oriented, as are most great goalies. "That's one thing that separates him from a lot of guys. He has that intangible. He is extremely coachable. He has tremendous work ethic. He has tremendous attention to detail, which is vital for a goaltender in today's game. And he's just got that great maturity for his age. There's never a day where he is not addressing the fundamentals of his game. I think every great goalie does that — has great daily patterns."

Those patterns got their start in Quebec, where so many of the game's best goalies have been spawned over the years. Born on April 4, 1979, in Montreal, Luongo was taken second overall by Val-d'Or in the 1995 Quebec Major Junior Hockey League midget draft. He spent parts of four QMJHL seasons with the Val-d'Or Foreurs and Acadie-Bathurst Titans. He broke into the league as a 16-year-old with the Foreurs and led them to a league-finals appearance in 1997–98. He was traded midway through the following season to the Titans, and also helped them reach the Memorial Cup tournament.

During his QMJHL career and the 1999 world junior tournament, Luongo's reputation reached almost legendary status as he drew comparisons to famous Quebecois puck-stopping predecessors such as Patrick Roy and Martin Brodeur.

Richard Martel, who coached Luongo for three seasons as a junior in Val-d'Or, remembers the 16-year-old rookie as "a nice kid" with a mental toughness that was unusual for his age. He was quiet, with "no nerves" and very mature, recalls Martel.

Luongo steadily improved after arriving in the QMJHL, Martel says, and truly arrived as a star when he backstopped Val-d'Or to a playoff win over the Granby Predateurs, coached by future Montreal Canadiens bench boss Michel Therrien.

"When the game was tied, Roberto Luongo was very strong," recalls Martel, who rates Luongo as the best goalie he has coached. "He has very nice concentration, before the game and during the game. He is very strong."

Luongo's junior record prompted the Islanders to draft him fourth overall in 1997, at the time the highest pick for a goalie in NHL history. But things didn't work out long-term on Long Island.

Luongo split his first pro season between the Islanders and their American Hockey League farm team, the Lowell [Massachusetts] Lock Monsters, going 7-14-1 with a 3.25 goals-against average as an NHL rookie. His NHL debut came on November 28, 1999, when he turned in 43 saves to beat the hometown Boston Bruins 2-1. Just a month later he would record his first NHL shutout, a 34-save, 3-0 blanking of the same Bruins.

That start apparently wasn't promising enough for Islanders general manager Mike Milbury. In 2000 Milbury broke his own record for selecting goalies high in the draft, picking Rick DiPietro, a Boston University freshman, No. 1 overall. In that same draft Milbury shipped Luongo and Jokinen, the No. 3 pick in 1997, to the Florida Panthers.

The Panthers put Luongo to work right away, playing him in 47 games during his first season in Miami. After a three-game stint in the minors with the Louisville Panthers of the American Hockey League, he went 4-3-5 over his final 11 games and finished with a save percentage of .920, seventh best in the league. He concluded the season with a respectable 2.44 average and a career-high five shutouts while posting a 12-24 record for the struggling Panthers.

During his second season in Florida Luongo appeared in 58 games and won 16 for the Panthers, a team that won only 22 games in total and finished in front of only two other clubs in the NHL. He posted a 2.77 average with four shutouts and a save percentage of .915, the same as Detroit's Vezina Trophy winner Dominik Hasek. But he missed the final 13 games of the season with a ligament tear in his right ankle.

Before Luongo's third season with the Panthers, Keenan told reporters that the next step along the line for Luongo was learning how to win, just as it was for the rest of his young lineup, which included eight NHL rookies.

Although he had his ups and down during the 2002–3 season, Luongo set a Panthers record with back-to-back January shutouts in 3-0 wins over Boston and Pittsburgh. He finished the season with a career-high six shutouts, a 2.71 average, a save percentage of .917 and a record of 20 wins, 34 losses and seven ties. Following the season, he joined Team Canada for the 2003 world tournament in Helsinki, where he backstopped his country to a 3-2 overtime victory over Sweden in the gold-medal game.

Luongo seems to be an ideal fit for a young team such as Florida, which has often needed a goalie to stand on his head in order to remain competitive in games. Luongo clearly relishes the chance to be that goalie. And he seems to realize that he's not going to be able to save the game every night, displaying a calm maturity while talking to reporters even after a difficult loss.

"You know, it's what I try to do every game, try to do my best, try to keep my team in the game," he says.

Perhaps Ian Clark, who coached Luongo in Florida, sums up the young goalie's growth the best: "There's no question that he has the ability to steal hockey games and I think he's demonstrated that for this young hockey club. I don't consider him a prospect any more. He's proven he's not a prospect. He's one of the premier netminders in the league." HYS

PAINTS
SUPERPRETZEL
79
BAUER
EASTON
EASTON

ANDREI MARKOV #79

MONTREAL CANADIENS • DEFENCE

Height: 6-0 Weight: 203 Born: December 20, 1978 — Voskresensk, Russia

Season	Team	GP	G	A	TP	PIM	+/-	Shots	Pct
2000–2001	Canadiens	63	6	17	23	18	-6	82	7.31
2001–2002	Canadiens	56	5	19	24	24	-1	73	6.84
2002–2003	Canadiens	79	13	24	37	34	13	159	8.17
NHL Totals		198	24	60	84	76	6	314	7.64

He is a man of few words, even in his mother tongue of Russian, which is probably the biggest reason many North American hockey fans don't know much about Andrei Markov. But the slick Montreal Canadiens' defenceman lets his game do the talking for him, and in just three seasons in the NHL that game has already made quite a statement.

Markov brought a nice assortment of offensive skills with him when he moved to Montreal from Moscow Dynamo in time for the 2000–1 NHL season. Since he has been in North America he has worked hard to become a seasoned defensive presence as well, giving the Canadiens one of the most promising young blueliners in the game.

Markov's NHL career was very nearly aborted, however. The language and cultural barriers made the transition so difficult that during his first year with the Canadiens organization he seriously considered returning to Russia.

"But then he reconsidered because his dream was to play hockey in the NHL and returning to Russia would make it almost impossible to come back and realize it," says Genadi Boguslavski, a Montreal-based journalist who covers the Canadiens for the Russian newspaper *Sovietsky Sport*. "Therefore he stayed and tried that much harder to play here and succeed."

Markov's English is still very limited and his rare comments in Montreal newspapers are typically only one or two words in length, but the emerging NHL defensive star agreed to be interviewed for *Hockey's Young Superstars* through Boguslavski.

The Canadiens' coaching staff has tried to help Markov with his English by having him room with veteran tough guy Gino Odjick when the team is on the road. Odjick learned to speak some Russian during his playing days with the Vancouver Canucks, when he became a good friend of star forward Pavel Bure.

Markov said he finds the transition to the NHL easier lately because the Canadiens have given him considerably more ice time than when he first arrived. That has helped to develop his skills and subsequently adapt to the North American game, which is played on a smaller ice surface, with different rules and more contact.

EXCUSE ME ... WAITER? Andrei Markov's girlfriend, Olga Svetsov, used to translate for the defenceman in almost every situation. "After a while, I decided he had to learn to do things for himself and I think that helped a lot," Svetsov told LES CANADIENS magazine during the 2002–3 season. "I figured if he got hungry enough, he would go ahead and order food himself, and he did. He had started to rely on me translating for him so much that I think it held him back."

His English has improved enough that he can now at least understand what the coaches want and is capable of grasping the plays they are trying to set up.

The six-foot, 203-pound defenceman still spends every off-season in Russia, where he trains with his former team, Moscow Dynamo.

But Markov is adapting to North American life. Rick Green, the Montreal assistant responsible for defencemen, told reporters recently that he was very surprised when Markov returned for his third NHL season and was able to communicate.

The Canadiens have also been pleasantly surprised by Markov's improvement on the ice. He has become one of the club's top defencemen and excels on the power play, certainly a good value for a 162nd-overall draft pick.

"Andrei has really developed into a good two-way defenceman this year," said Trevor Timmins, the Canadiens' director of player personnel, midway through the 2002–3 NHL season. "I would say this has been his breakthrough season."

"He's still a young defenceman, but he's playing with a lot of confidence," Markov's defensive partner, Craig Rivet, told the Montreal *Gazette*. "He's always had the offensive skills. You can't take those away from someone, and he has learned that when we're playing five-on-five, defence has to come first."

Andrei Markov's hockey education began a world away from Montreal and the glitzy arenas of the NHL. He was born on December 20, 1979, in Voskresensk, Russia, a city of about 90,000 located 80 kilometres from Moscow. A relatively anonymous place, Voskresensk has nevertheless quietly developed a reputation as a hockey factory after producing the likes of NHLers Igor Larionov, Sergei Berezin, Valerie Zelepukin and Vyacheslav Kozlov. The town has even played host to a visit from the Stanley Cup. In 1997, after the Detroit Red Wings captured the NHL championship, Larionov and Kozlov took the fabled hockey silverware home to Voskresensk in the off-season. The city is represented by the hockey team Khimik Voskresensk, formerly of the Soviet elite league. Although he was not at first a fan of Khimik, Andrei gradually became one as he grew older.

Markov began skating at age five but didn't play hockey until he was eight, when his parents, Viktor and Raisa, began taking him to the local hockey school in Voskresensk — the Children Junior Sporting School of Khimik — whose most famous alumnus is Larionov.

Andrei also enjoyed boxing and played basketball as a youngster before concentrating solely on hockey. He recalls dropping out of the hockey school for a week or two during his teen years, but he quickly returned to it after he realized his deep love for the game and his desire to play hockey as a career.

During this period his first coach was Anatoly Kozlov, father of Atlanta Thrashers' centre Vyacheslav Kozlov. The elder Kozlov served as a mentor to Andrei while he was with the Voskresensk hockey school.

At just 16, Markov got a try out with Khimik Voskresensk and, a year later, he made the club's elite professional squad. He spent three seasons there, recording eight goals and four assists in 43 games during his second season and following that up with 10 goals and five assists a year later.

His ice time grew dramatically in his second season with Khimik after he switched positions, a move that ultimately paved the way for his NHL career. Incoming Voskresensk coach Valerie Nikitin suggested Markov move full-time from centre to defence, where he would see much more ice time.

During that season Markov also played for the Russian team at the world junior championships. He made the national side again the following year, when he was chosen as an all-star at the 1998 world junior tournament.

That performance was enough for the Canadiens to use their sixth pick, 162nd overall, on the Russian defenceman in the 1998 NHL entry draft. But he didn't join Montreal right away, instead opting to jump to the powerful Russian club Moscow Dynamo for two seasons in the Russian Superligue.

In his first season with Dynamo, Markov recorded 10 goals and 11 assists in 38 elite league games and another seven goals and five assists in 12 Euro Hockey League contests. With Dynamo, Markov worked under coach Zinetula Bilyaletdinov, whom he credits for helping to develop his skills further and turn him into the player he is today.

The Canadiens wanted him to join their NHL lineup after that season but Markov remained to fulfill his two-year contract with Dynamo, posting his best Russian season with 11 goals and 23 points in 29 games in 1999–2000 to lead all Superligue defencemen in scoring.

He was selected the best defenceman and also won the Golden Helmet award as the most valuable player in the Russian elite league in each of his two seasons with Dynamo.

He also became a fan favourite, particularly in the 11,000-seat Luzhniki Sports Palace, as he led Dynamo to the Superligue regular-season championship. He was considered by many the best Russian player outside the NHL.

The most memorable moment of Markov's career in his homeland was a strange goal he scored in the dying seconds of the deciding game of the Superligue playoff finals. It came on a slapshot from beside his own goal, travelled the length of the ice and beat the glove hand of Boris Tortunov to allow Dynamo to tie Metallurg Magnitogorsk 1-1 and send the game into overtime. However, Dynamo lost the game and the championship in the extra session.

Leaving Russia to play in the NHL meant getting used to a faster style of play and a narrower ice surface. It also meant a huge cultural shift and leaving behind his parents and sister, Galina, who all still live in Voskresensk.

Although he enjoyed hockey in Russia, Markov says he loves playing in the NHL because the best hockey players in the world are part of the league.

"For him, it is very important to respect the players on the other team," explains Boguslavski. "When playing against players such as [Mario] Lemieux and [Mats] Sundin, the first couple of shifts are usually nerve-racking but, as the game progresses, the nervousness goes away and he gets into the rhythm of the game."

During the season Markov lives with his girlfriend, Olga Svetsov, in Montreal. He still prefers Russian food to North American cuisine, opting to visit Russian restaurants.

Markov's biggest objective in hockey is a team-oriented one — to win a Stanley Cup, with the Canadiens or another club. In only three NHL seasons he has already reached some significant personal milestones despite splitting time between the Canadiens and their American Hockey League farm club, the Quebec Citadelles, during his first two years.

When he was sent down to Quebec late in his rookie season, partially because of his language difficulties, he took it hard. "It was extremely tough on him," Olga told *Les Canadiens* magazine. "It really hurt his confidence. But when you get to know Andrei, you find out that if he wants something he will stop at nothing to make it happen."

"HE PLAYS WITH a lot of drive. He sees the ice very well, he moves the puck very effectively and he's got a great shot." — Montreal Canadiens head scout Trevor Timmins, on Andrei Markov

In 63 NHL games during his rookie season Markov recorded an impressive 23 points, including six goals. In his second campaign he had 24 points in seven fewer games. In both seasons he averaged about 17 minutes a game in ice time. He improved from a minus-6 in his first season with the Canadiens to a minus-1 in the second year.

Markov enjoyed a breakthrough season in 2002–3, though the Canadiens struggled as a team and missed the playoffs. He finished with 13 goals and 24 assists, while going an impressive plus-13 — all career bests — over 79 games.

"He plays with a lot of drive," says Trevor Timmins, the Canadiens head scout who has been analyzing pro hockey players for more than 11 years. "He sees the ice very well, he moves the puck very effectively and he's got a great shot."

Markov has quickly improved to the point where he is easily one of the top four defencemen playing for the Canadiens. "He's a mid-range defenceman [in the NHL] and working his way up there," Timmins says.

Some pro hockey observers, including his teammates, were disappointed that Markov was overlooked for the Eastern Conference lineup in the 53rd NHL All-Star Game.

"He's on the brink of stardom," former Canadiens and current Boston Bruins goalie Jeff Hackett told the Montreal *Gazette* as the All-Star break neared.

"[Markov] should have been added to the team," added Canadiens' captain Saku Koivu, himself an All-Star, in the same *Gazette* article.

Markov would appear to have an All-Star season or two in front of him as his promising career continues in the NHL. The young Russian still might not have a lot to say off the ice, but his game is clearly speaking for itself. HYS

PATRICK MARLEAU #12

SAN JOSE SHARKS • CENTRE

Height: 6-2 Weight: 210 Born: September 15, 1979 – Aneroid, SK

Season	Team	GP	G	A	TP	PIM	+/-	Shots	Pct
1997–1998	Sharks	74	13	19	32	14	5	90	14.44
1998–1999	Sharks	81	21	24	45	24	10	134	15.67
1999–2000	Sharks	81	17	23	40	36	-9	161	10.55
2000–2001	Sharks	81	25	27	52	22	7	146	17.12
2001–2002	Sharks	79	21	23	44	40	9	121	17.35
2002–2003	Sharks	82	28	29	57	33	-10	172	16.27
NHL Totals		478	125	145	270	169	12	824	15.16

His story reads like a slice of pure Canadiana: Youngster learns how to skate like the wind atop a frozen pond on the south Saskatchewan prairie. Youngster doesn't stop skating until he reaches the NHL.

But the tale of Patrick Marleau isn't quite so simple. Yes, he honed his skating skills atop a dugout on the family's 1,600-acre farm. And, yes, he was what most people would call a natural. But Marleau's rise to the NHL also took plenty of hard work and considerable sacrifice.

Marleau grew up on the family farm just outside the tiny town of Aneroid, population 85. He was just 13 when his family realized he should leave home to pursue his dream of playing hockey at the highest level.

That's when young Patrick moved to Swift Current, an hour's drive north from the family's mixed cattle and grain operation. He went to live with his grandmother, Laurette, so that he could play bantam hockey in the comparatively larger Saskatchewan centre.

"It was tough," recalls Denis Marleau, his father. "But you could tell he had a dream. So we kind of had to follow through."

Denis knew that if he and his wife, Jeanette, didn't allow and encourage their youngest son to make the move, he might not reach his potential as a hockey player. "I knew we had to do this," he says, "or later on it would have come back to haunt me. I would have always thought: 'I wonder what would have happened ...'"

No need to wonder any more. A decade later, Patrick Marleau is one of the most talented young players in the NHL, using his God-given speed to tear up the ice for the San Jose Sharks. His special gift for the game is evident to anybody who watches him now. And while it wasn't quite so obvious back in Aneroid, there were definitely early signs.

Denis Marleau remembers young Patrick skating for hours on the pond on the farm that has been worked by his family for generations. He remembers taking Patrick to afternoons on the Aneroid rink, a modest indoor facility with natural ice, often colder inside than it is outside. "That's one of the great things about these small towns," Denis says. "You can go to the ice just about any time and get on there. There are no schedules like in the bigger places."

Denis remembers his son's first skate in that arena, where the ice often becomes wet and heavy when the temperature gets too high. It was like that on their first visit, when Patrick was about four years old. Denis took a chair for his son to hang onto, in case he had problems standing up. That arrangement didn't last long. Even then, the youngster didn't want anything slowing him down.

"YOU WANT TO have an impact on every game, whether you're scoring points or not." —Patrick Marleau

"He went halfway around that ice. He didn't even get around once and then he cut diagonally over to me," Denis recalls. "He said, 'Dad, I don't want to push this.' Then he took off and he's never looked back."

Patrick loved hockey, but he loved baseball, too, playing pitcher and every other position on the diamond with the other kids from Aneroid. "You play just about every position when there are only nine kids around," he laughs.

Young Patrick was a natural athlete, with a smooth, quiet confidence. Denis Marleau remembers his son interacting with the quarter horses the family raised for a while. While nobody else could manage to get close to the flighty colts, Patrick would simply stick out his hand and they would go to him.

He was a strong skater right from the beginning, getting a solid base in power skating and even figure skating along with his older siblings, Denise and Richard. When Patrick started playing organized hockey at age six, he was immediately a dominant player in Aneroid. His dad coached him until the second year of peewee, when the Marleaus decided their boy would be better off playing on a Swift Current team.

During that first season away, Denis and Patrick made the commute to Swift Current for practices and games. One of the peewee team's regular practices was a 6 a.m. weekday start. Denis and Patrick would drive to Swift Current the night before, stay at his grandmother's house, attend practice in the morning and then be back in Aneroid in time for school.

The next year, Patrick moved into Swift Current and lived with his grandmother during his second season of bantam, when he recorded an incredible 95 goals and 167 points in 53 games. He remained there for a season of AAA midget as well. Then it was time for a much bigger move, relocating from Swift Current to the major West Coast centre of

Seattle to play with the Western Hockey League's Thunderbirds. He wasn't even 16 when he made that decision.

The move was a big one for everybody in the family. Jeanette, a schoolteacher at a Hutterite colony near Aneroid, had seen other children leave their homes early to play hockey and had sworn she would never allow her boy to do that. She eventually relented, but Denis recalls plenty of long-distance phone calls during that first year Patrick was in Seattle.

Despite being barely 16, Patrick posted 32 goals and 74 points for the Thunderbirds in his rookie WHL season, providing himself with the first inkling that he might actually be able to one day realize his dream of making the NHL.

Seattle general manager Russ Farwell remembers a quiet kid coming from small-town Saskatchewan to quickly become a star in the WHL — quiet, but at the same time determined and self-confident. Patrick wasn't the type of player whom you rode or hounded into performing, Farwell recalls, but rather one who responded to challenges laid out for him.

"He was a man by the time he came here at 16," Farwell says. "And he was just blessed with a great set of wheels. When you skate like that, it gives you that much more time on the ice."

That speed helped Marleau raise his offensive numbers dramatically during his draft year. In just his second season with the Thunderbirds, he piled up 51 goals and 125 points and was runner-up to Peter Schaefer of the Brandon Wheat Kings for Western Hockey League player-of-the-year honours. He led the league in shorthanded goals and in the playoffs helped Seattle reach the WHL championship series.

Marleau's numbers at such a young age, his size (six foot two, 190 pounds) and, of course, his skating ability turned him into a top prospect for the 1997 NHL draft. Because his birthday is on September 15 he was eligible for that year's draft by just a single day, making him the youngest possible age for any player to be selected by an NHL team.

That didn't detract from the interest in him, however. On the contrary, player agents were beginning to phone the Marleau farm in Aneroid as often as three times a night by that spring. Scouts were visiting both Seattle and the farm to check out the youngster.

By the time draft day arrived in Pittsburgh in June, Marleau was a name near the top of many teams' lists. And with his family contingent in the stands at Melion Arena numbering 14, Patrick was taken second overall in the draft by the San Jose Sharks, behind only Joe Thornton of the Sault Ste. Marie Greyhounds, who went No. 1 to the Boston Bruins.

Russ Farwell remembers attending a post-draft celebration in Aneroid that drew hundreds of people. "The entire town was there and more," he says. "It was amazing. And Pat handled that as well as any guy could have. He was nice to everyone, from the young kids to the little old ladies."

Both Farwell and Denis Marleau felt Patrick would be back in Seattle for another year of junior. But the Sharks surprised them by keeping the 18-year-old rookie in their lineup, making him one of the youngest NHLers in history.

CCM
JOFA
12

The Sharks were light in talent at the centre position and they felt Marleau could contribute right away, even if he was the youngest player in the NHL that season. "You can talk about his age all you want," Sharks coach Darryl Sutter told the San Francisco *Examiner* before the season started. "He's as skilled as anyone here. He's as big as anyone here."

Nevertheless, it was certainly a huge transition for Marleau, stepping from junior right into pro hockey's finest circuit at such a young age. But helping with that adjustment was Sharks veteran goaltender Kelly Hrudey, now a commentator for *Hockey Night in Canada.* Hrudey took Patrick into his home for the first season and invited the rookie to live with his family.

Coach Darryl Sutter tried to ease the youngster into the NHL, initially limiting his playing time and keeping him off the ice when games were out of reach and things tended to get really rough. His other teammates with the Sharks also helped. Marleau likens the experience to joining one big, extended family. "Hockey players, no matter what their age, they're all just big kids," he laughs.

On the ice Marleau turned in a decent rookie season, scoring 13 goals and finishing with 32 points to place fourth in scoring among first-year players. His numbers jumped to 21 goals and 45 points the next year and his production remained at about that level for the following three seasons as he continued to learn on the fly in the NHL. Marleau's skating

AN EARLY START

Patrick Marleau's first NHL goal, on October 19, 1997, against the Phoenix Coyotes, made him the second-youngest player to score in the regular season since those records have been kept by the league. Only Grant Mulvey, who scored for the Chicago Black Hawks in 1974, was younger. Marleau also managed to play his 400th game earlier than any other player in league history.

ability was recognized during the 1999–2000 season when he won the fastest skater contest, part of the super skills competition, during the midseason NHL All-Star festivities.

The youngster had to work hard, as any young player does, so that he wouldn't be a defensive liability to the Sharks. But the biggest overall adjustment to the NHL at such a young age was learning to bring the same intensity to the ice every night. Consistency is a goal Marleau set his sights on. "I guess that consistency doesn't always have to do with [offensive] numbers, though," he cautions. "You want to have an impact on every game, whether you're scoring points or not."

Marleau seemed to hit his stride as an NHLer near the end of his fifth season. He finished the 2001–2 campaign with a flourish, recording 16 points over his final 10 games, including 10 goals. He was also the Sharks' leading scorer during the ensuing playoffs, with 11 points.

He picked up where he left off during his sixth season, although that year also brought some turmoil to the Sharks as Darryl Sutter, Marleau's head coach since he broke into the NHL, was fired. Nevertheless, he managed to produce consistent numbers for most of the season and, as a result, he enjoyed a breakout campaign, scoring 28 goals and 29 assists for 57 points — all career bests — playing on a dangerous line with Finnish scoring star Teemu Selanne.

"I think he's going to be one of the best players to ever play this game," Selanne told the San Francisco *Chronicle* early in Marleau's sixth season. "He has all the tools and he's a great kid."

When assessing Marleau's career, many forget just how young he still is. He had already played six full NHL seasons before celebrating his 24th birthday.

"He's just showing us the tip of his talents," says Russ Farwell, who rates Marleau as a better pure talent than either Petr Nedved or Trevor Linden, two other stars he handled as juniors. "As he matures and gains confidence, I think there's no limit to his upside." HYS

DEREK MORRIS #53

COLORADO AVALANCHE • DEFENCE

Height: 6-0 Weight: 210 Born: August 24, 1978 – Edmonton

Season	Team	GP	G	A	TP	PIM	+/-	Shots	Pct
1997–1998	Flames	82	9	20	29	88	1	120	7.5
1998–1999	Flames	71	7	27	34	73	4	150	4.66
1999–2000	Flames	78	9	29	38	80	2	193	4.66
2000–2001	Flames	51	5	23	28	56	-15	142	3.52
2001–2002	Flames	61	4	30	34	88	-4	166	2.40
2002–2003	Avalanche	75	11	37	48	68	16	191	5.75
NHL Totals		418	45	166	211	453	4	962	4.67

For many major junior hockey prospects in Canada, the dream dies at the annual intrasquad game, which typically divides the remaining players into two teams and signals the end of training camp. Those teens who aren't good enough, or old enough, or big enough, are sent home, carrying their equipment bags and heavy hearts.

With defenceman Derek Morris, there was a slight twist to the storyline. After his first training camp with the Regina Pats and after playing in the WHL team's annual Blue-White intrasquad scrimmage, the 17-year-old kid from Sylvan Lake, Alberta, sent himself home. Pats' general manager Brent Parker remembers it well. It was his first season running the Regina club and he had been impressed with Derek's play during camp. But minutes after the intrasquad game ended, Parker was informed by the coaching staff that he had better get out to the parking lot and talk to the youngster.

"Derek didn't think that he was good enough, to the point he actually left the team at the end of training camp," Parker recalls.

Morris returned home to Sylvan Lake with his dad, Terry, a former Edmonton police officer. Parker and the Pats' coaching staff were surprised at his decision, but they decided to give the youngster some time to reconsider. His parents did, too. The Morris family is extremely close and Terry Morris knew that his son was probably having trouble coming to terms with the idea of leaving home.

"He wanted to go, but he didn't know if he was quite ready yet," Terry says now. "We came back from Regina and just kind of let him have his space."

After his return home, Derek's midget coach in Red Deer, Dan MacDonald, helped steer the youngster toward the WHL, assuring him that he was ready to make the step up to hockey's next level.

EASTON

A couple of weeks after leaving the Pats, Derek Morris called Brent Parker in Regina. "Would it be okay if I came back?" he asked. It was more than okay with the Pats, who had been pleased with his play during training camp. "I think everything had been just happening so fast and it spooked him a little bit," Parker says.

Derek flew back to Regina — on his own, this time. It was difficult to say goodbye and not just for the teenager. "For me, it was really hard," Terry Morris says. "I had many sleepless nights that first month, until I met his billets and saw that they were a good family and realized it was a top-notch organization."

Brent Parker and his head coach with the Pats at the time, former NHLer Rich Preston, decided the best plan was to ease the rookie into the WHL. But by the second period of his first game with Regina, Preston already had Morris killing penalties and playing on the first power-play unit. Parker remembers asking his coach what had happened to their plan for the rookie. "It's pretty tough to ease him in when he's your best player," the coach replied. That story sums up the personality of Derek Morris, who seems to take nothing for granted on the ice.

"That's a rarity, unfortunately," Parker says. "You've got too many players now who are the exact opposite. They expect everything to be handed to them. Derek felt all along that he had to earn everything he was getting and he did."

Derek Morris was born in Edmonton on August 24, 1978. When he was about three years old the family moved south to Sylvan Lake, a quiet cottage town of about 5,000 that sits roughly halfway between Calgary and Edmonton. He was always a defenceman, following in the footsteps of his father, who first took him skating on an outdoor rink in Edmonton before he had turned four. "My dad took me out when I was young and I've just been hooked ever since," he says.

He began playing organized hockey just a year later. Terry Morris coached Derek through minor hockey in Sylvan Lake until he reached the peewee level.

"My father played defence and I could skate backward, so they just kind of threw me back there," Derek explains. He has been on the blue line ever since, eventually developing into one of the top young defencemen in the NHL.

Still, he remembers being pretty ordinary when he first started playing the game. "I don't think I was anything special," he says. His father remembers it a little differently: Terry says Derek was always one of the better players in his age group and always a good skater. At times, he was called up to Sylvan Lake's older teams on a fill-in basis. Like Terry's two other sons, Derek was a natural athlete at just about anything, although hockey was his only serious, competitive sport.

By the time he approached junior age there was plenty of interest in Derek's talents, particularly after he was named top defenceman at the 1995 Air Canada Cup national midget championship while playing for Red Deer, a city about a 15-minute drive west of his home.

And after that one standout season of midget as a 16-year-old — when he amassed 41 points in 31 games — it was time to move up. That meant leaving his parents, Terry and

A TOWN DIVIDED

If you're from Sylvan Lake, Alberta, chances are you line up on either one side or the other. The small resort town is about halfway between Edmonton and Calgary, and your NHL team of choice is either the Oilers or the Flames. Young Derek Morris cheered for the Oilers, somewhat ironic since he would eventually end up being drafted by the Flames. "Growing up, obviously, Paul Coffey was the big defenceman [to follow] in Alberta," Morris says now. "But as I got older, I kind of liked the way Chris Chelios played at both ends of the ice."

Wendy, his older sister, Brandie, and two younger brothers, Blair and Garrett. To play in the WHL he joined the Pats in Regina, about a five-hour drive from home.

While the transition was initially difficult, Morris enjoyed his two seasons with the Pats and the WHL club enjoyed having him in its lineup. The 17-year-old who at the beginning of the season hadn't considered himself ready to play on the team wound up with eight goals and 52 points in 67 games in that rookie campaign.

Those numbers were good enough to earn the attention of NHL scouts leading up to the 1996 entry draft. The entire Morris family attended the event, held in St. Louis. Derek had been ranked as a third- or fourth-rounder early on, but his stock rose as several teams interviewed him before draft day. By the time it finally arrived, he had climbed all the way to 13th spot overall, where he was selected by Calgary.

"MY FATHER PLAYED defence and I could skate backward, so they just kind of threw me back there." — Derek Morris

Morris returned to Regina for a final season of junior hockey, however. Back with the Pats, and playing alongside future NHLer Brad Stuart on the power play, he justified Calgary's high opinion of him by scoring 18 times and adding 57 assists to top all WHL defencemen with 75 points. During that second junior season, he piled up 180 minutes in penalties, proving that he was comfortable with the rough going as well.

"I think it was his confidence increasing as much as anything — playing against the premier defencemen in our league and realizing that he was one of them," Parker says of Morris' growth while he was in Regina.

Following the WHL season, Morris made his professional debut with Calgary's farm club, the Saint John Flames of the American Hockey League, posting six assists in seven regular-season games and five playoff contests combined.

The Pats hoped to get Morris back the next season, but the 19-year-old made the jump directly to the NHL, playing all 82 games with the Flames and finishing with an impressive 29 points, including nine goals, in his rookie year. Those numbers were enough to earn a spot on the NHL All-Rookie team, but even as that season progressed he still wasn't completely sure he would make a long-term living at the game. "My whole first year with the Flames, I played thinking I was about to be sent back to junior," he recalls.

He needn't have worried. By the time he reached his 25th birthday he had already completed six full NHL seasons. In the process, he has become one of the league's top point producers on the blue line, surpassing the 30-point plateau in each of the last two seasons. As well, he has evolved into a workhorse on defence, averaging close to 25 minutes of ice time per game over the last four seasons.

He has also discovered, as most NHLers do, that the game is a business and that players are commodities. For Morris, that hit home on October 1, 2002, just days before he was about to start his sixth season with the Flames and shortly after getting married in Banff.

That's when he learned he was part of a blockbuster preseason trade with the Colorado Avalanche that sent him, Jeff Shantz and Dean McAmmond to Denver in exchange for Chris Drury and Stephane Yelle. Reeling from the news, his first call was to Flames teammate Jarome Iginla, with whom he'd hoped to eventually lead Calgary back into the playoffs.

"It was a shock," Morris says now. "I wanted to stay there in Calgary my whole career ... As an NHL player, I guess you kind of expect it, but at the same time you don't expect it."

While the trade was difficult for his wife, Jodie, and their two preschool boys, Traiten and Presley, going to the Avalanche was definitely positive for Morris. Denver isn't far from Alberta, where he and his family continue to maintain a cabin on Sylvan Lake. And in the Avalanche he was joining a veteran defensive corps and a franchise that is a perennial Stanley Cup contender. He went from a situation where he was the prime defender in Calgary to being part of one of the strongest blue line contingents in the league.

In Colorado he has been fortunate enough to play with rock-solid Adam Foote as well as Rob Blake, a talented offensive rearguard with whom he was already familiar as a teammate on Team Canada at the 1999 world championships. "It's great in Colorado," Morris says. "All the defencemen here are so much fun to play with. Everybody feeds off one another. It's a tight, tight team. That's probably why they've been so successful."

He got off to a solid start with the Avs, posting career bests of 11 goals and 48 points during the 2002–3 season. He also managed a plus-16 rating for the year, easily the finest of his career. Those numbers came even though the 24-year-old defenceman missed a handful of games after requiring surgery to repair a blowout fracture of the orbit bone around his right eye, caused by a punch during a fight with David Ling of the Columbus Blue Jackets. In the first playoff appearance of his NHL career, Morris had three assists in seven games as the Avalanche fell victim to the Anaheim Mighty Ducks in a disappointing first-round upset.

Teammates and coaches have tagged Morris as a future winner of the Norris Trophy, the award annually given to the NHL's top defenceman. Brent Parker says that although Derek's offensive skills are what first grab your attention, "he's a better defensive player than people give him credit for."

"It doesn't surprise me that he's been able to do what he's done [at the NHL level]," Parker says. "And I think that we're just seeing the tip of the iceberg."

Terry Morris admits that, even after all his son's years in the big leagues, "you still find yourself a bit in awe of what's happened." But he is proud that Derek hasn't been changed by NHL success. He always told his son to enjoy riding the wave of pro sports and never to take anything for granted.

"Nothing has gone to his head," Terry says. "That's not his way. Derek keeps a low-profile image. You would never know he was a professional hockey player." HYS

61

RICK NASH #61

COLUMBUS BLUE JACKETS • LEFT WING

Height: 6-3 Weight: 202 Born: June 16, 1984 – Brampton, ON

Season	Team	GP	G	A	TP	PIM	+/-	Shots	Pct
2002–2003	Blue Jackets	74	17	22	39	78	-27	154	11.03
NHL Totals		74	17	22	39	78	-27	154	11.03

For many North Americans, 18 is an age to enter university, start learning a trade, take that first full-time job or head off to explore the world. It's an age when most of us are just beginning to pursue our dreams. At 18 Rick Nash was already living his, as a teenage power forward in the NHL.

Just a few months after he was riding junior hockey buses through the wilds of Ontario with the London Knights, Nash found himself dashing up the left wing for the Columbus Blue Jackets and a member in good standing of the planet's premier puck league.

"It all just seems like a pretty big whirlwind," the Brampton, Ontario, youngster admitted midway through his rookie NHL season.

He no longer billets in the home of Joe and Sue Phillips, as he did back in London. Instead, he lives on his own in a townhouse in the Ohio capital and drives a brand new Trail Blazer. He rides in charter airplanes and stays in first-class hotels. He routinely visits major cities in every part of North America and plays against the same NHL stars he watched while growing up. Yes, there have been a few changes in Rick Nash's life.

"It's a lot different — kind of a different lifestyle," Nash laughs. "It's exciting. It's everything that I dreamed of growing up. I'm really enjoying it."

Nash was born and raised in Brampton, a suburb of Toronto, where the Maple Leafs are the undisputed sports kings. As a hockey-crazy kid he loved watching Toronto captain Mats Sundin, even though his own game is patterned more after Detroit Red Wings' power forward Brendan Shanahan.

Rick was only two when his father, Jamie, and older brother, James, first took him skating on a frozen pond on a vacant piece of land near the family's house. "He was a good skater," says his mother, Liz Nash. "He was skating backwards before most of the other kids were skating forwards."

He was also a terrific minor-hockey player, always one of the best on the select teams for which he played. But it's a long way from minor-hockey star to the NHL. "I kind of always wished it for him and thought he was really good," says his mom, "but I never dreamed of the NHL."

Besides hockey, Nash played soccer, baseball and lacrosse, the latter a sport in which his hand-eye coordination enabled him to play goalie. He particularly enjoyed lacrosse, suiting up in both the box and field versions of the sport as a youngster. "That's all the kids did was sports," Liz Nash says. "We lived at the arena, summer and winter."

A growth spurt around the age of 14, combined with his already prodigious puck skills, left Rick Nash in high demand with Ontario Hockey League teams as a bantam. The London Knights selected him fourth overall in the OHL bantam draft. "He was our guy," recalls Knights head coach and team owner Dale Hunter, a veteran of 19 NHL seasons himself.

Hunter liked Nash's skating skills. He noticed that, despite his gangly appearance, the kid possessed deceptive speed and rarely was beaten to the puck by anybody. "He can really skate," thought the coach the first time he watched Nash.

"EVERYBODY SAID he'd probably go third before the draft. After he was picked No. 1, I didn't even cry because I was in such shock." — Liz Nash, on her son Rick's NHL draft day

But what caught the eyes of the Knights brass was the youngster's special blend of talent and team play. During one bantam game that Hunter witnessed, he was taken by a single sequence. Late in that game, Nash already had two goals but he passed up a golden chance for a hat trick with an empty net staring at him. Instead of shooting, he slid the puck over so a teammate could score the goal.

"That told us that not only was he a great player, he was also a team player," Hunter says. "Everybody looks for goal scorers, but he was also very unselfish, passed the puck, saw the ice well."

Moving to London to play junior meant leaving the North Brampton home where Rick had lived with his mom since he was born. For Liz, it meant a 90-minute drive separating her from her youngest son. "I was devastated," she recalls. "I thought, 'Who's going to look after him?' And I guess for a kid in that situation you've really got to grow up fast."

Nash joined the Knights as a young 16-year-old — his birthday is in June — but nevertheless posted 31 goals and 35 assists in 58 games to capture OHL rookie-of-the-year honours and make the Canadian Hockey League all-rookie team as well.

The next season he topped that performance by recording 72 points, including 32 goals, over four fewer games. The scouts loved those numbers, but they also loved these ones: six foot three and 188 pounds ... and still growing by the day. They also loved the fact that Nash was a player whom the puck seemed to follow around. He possessed the sort of intuition for the bounces that can't be imparted by a coach.

"It wasn't really until the last year of junior, when the first Central Scouting list (which rates upcoming draft picks) came out, that I started seriously thinking about it," Nash says. "That was the first time I said to myself that I could actually make a career out of this. I mean, it was always my dream growing up to play in the NHL, but I knew hardly anybody — like one in 1,000 players — actually makes it."

Rick Nash would turn out to be that one. In fact, when the June 22 NHL entry draft was held in Toronto he was the No. 1 selection overall. In a move that took observers by surprise, the Blue Jackets engineered a draft-day trade that allowed them to vault from the No. 3 pick overall to the top spot specifically so they could secure the London star.

The turn of events left the Nash family, who had showed up in full force at the Air Canada Centre for the draft, a little stunned. "Everybody said he'd probably go third before the draft," Liz Nash says now. "After he was picked No. 1, I didn't even cry because I was in such shock."

Columbus general manager Doug MacLean wanted to ensure he landed Nash — so much so that he made the necessary deal with the Florida Panthers. The Panthers were set on picking Jay Bouwmeester, the rangy Medicine Hat defenceman who had widely been expected to be the draft's No. 1 selection. But by the time the dust settled, he had gone third. Sandwiched between Nash and Bouwmeester was highly rated Finnish goaltender Kari Lehtonen, who went to the Atlanta Thrashers.

"It was amazing," Nash told reporters immediately after the draft. "I was thinking Bouwmeester would go first and then they announced the trade and my stomach just dropped. I still didn't know what would happen. It was like a roller coaster."

"I didn't expect to go No. 1 in the draft at all," Nash says now. "Columbus showed a lot of faith in me. Now I've got to repay them."

It's that kind of attitude that had Blue Jackets teammates and coaches raving about Nash during his rookie season, when he stepped directly into the NHL and made an immediate impact as a teenager. He finished with 17 goals and 22 assists, along with 78 penalty minutes. He was also selected for the NHL's Young Stars game on February 1 in Sunrise, Florida, and scored a pair of goals in the high-profile showcase.

"He's always shown the ability to raise his game to another level," Dale Hunter says. "That's what he's already doing in the National Hockey League. That's what he did in that Young Stars game."

Nash seems pleased simply to have been able to stick with the Blue Jackets at such a young age. Though he eventually signed a three-year contract that pays $1.185 million US annually and could be worth more than $12 million US including incentives, he didn't know what to expect heading into his first NHL training camp. He said the Blue Jackets made no guarantees that he would even remain in Columbus. He believed there was a very real chance that he could be sent back to London for a third OHL season, so being in the NHL as a teenager is a bonus he is enjoying. Hunter said the Knights were hoping to get Nash back for one more year in the OHL, but they certainly weren't counting on it. "He deserves to be

> **A DANDY DEBUT**
> Rick Nash's rookie season got off to the kind of start that most NHL players only fantasize about. With his parents and brother in the stands of Nationwide Arena, he scored a goal on a rebound as his Columbus Blue Jackets beat the Chicago Blackhawks 2-1 on October 10, 2002. "It was exciting playing my first game in the NHL," Nash recalls. "The goal just made it everything I ever dreamed of. It was a great night. I'd never throw it back for anything."

there [in the NHL]," Hunter says. "Unfortunately for us, we could have used him."

Nash was wise enough not to place any major expectations on himself once he did make the NHL club. He didn't make any point projections for his rookie season, mainly because he didn't know what to expect. "I had shorter goals this year," he says. "I tried to work hard each period, each shift."

The Blue Jackets plan to build their franchise around Nash, a nice combination of physicality and finesse. He is an excellent puckhandler and shooter who doesn't shy away from the heavygoing in the corners. He also has a long reach some have compared to that of Mario Lemieux, which allows him to make surprising moves on defenders.

"The first thing I noticed is he's such a dangerous one-on-one player at the age of 18," said 13-year NHL veteran and Blue Jackets teammate Geoff Sanderson, midway through Nash's rookie season. "I've never seen an 18-year-old who can beat guys one-on-one like he can. He's got a really long reach and he's a really deceptive skater. He's got agility and when he winds it up he can handle that puck. To beat guys one-on-one at 18 years of age is very impressive in the NHL and he's going to be a very dangerous player."

Blue Jackets centre Andrew Cassels, a 14-year NHL veteran, says Nash will only get better as he gets bigger and stronger and learns the intricacies of positional play in the NHL. "You don't get away with the things you can get away with in junior. It's going to cost you sometimes and he's going to learn that and he's just going to get better every game and every year."

Sanderson says Nash will have to improve defensively — he finished a dismal minus-27 for his rookie season. "But that goes for everybody, first year in the league or not. That can be taught, though. He's got everything that can not be taught by any coach."

Nash says the transition to the NHL lifestyle hasn't been a problem, either. "I don't think it's a big adjustment," he says. "It's not like in junior, where we were riding buses for six hours and then getting off the bus to play that same evening. Now we're flying in the night before."

Although he made a relatively smooth step up, there were still plenty of lessons to learn in the NHL in that rookie season. At times, Nash found himself getting pushed off the puck.

"Guys are, like, 30-year-old men and they just throw you around in the corners," he says of the big jump from junior hockey. "And the speed of the game is unbelievable. But the guys here on the team have helped me out a lot."

He has also had to learn about the cutthroat side of the game. Dave King, his first NHL coach and the first coach in Columbus franchise history, was fired by the Blue Jackets before the All-Star break of this rookie season. But general manager Doug MacLean, who took over behind the bench for King, also seemed pleased with Nash's development and maturity. Midway through the season, he already felt comfortable putting him on the ice in just about any situation.

TPS

"He's that type of kid," MacLean says. "He's been solid defensively, the vets love him — the kid's got a chance to be a great young player in the league."

Nash has made a concentrated attempt to beef up, too, going from 188 pounds to 202 by midway through his rookie season. "My goal is to eventually play about six foot four and 220 pounds," he says. "I'm still 18. I still have some growing to do."

Many believe he will eventually be one of the toughest forwards in the NHL. "He has that burst of speed and the ability to score, like Michel Goulet," says Dale Hunter, comparing his former junior star to one of his more illustrious former NHL teammates.

"You wait until he fills out in the NHL. He'll add 15 to 20 pounds and then you've got a horse."

MacLean says Nash possesses great vision on the ice and rarely loses a race for the puck. "People question his skating but this guy has a chance to be a great skater. He has tremendous lateral mobility, he jumps on loose pucks, he sees the ice very well, he's got a great set of hands."

Perhaps the quality about Nash the rookie that most surprised teammates, however, was his maturity. Fellow Blue Jackets, who had watched an 18-year-old rewarded with more than a million dollars a season before he had even played a minute in the NHL, found themselves describing the new kid in the dressing room as "classy."

"He's a shy guy and he knows he's got all this pressure and expectations on him and he's just feeling his way through his first year here," says Geoff Sanderson. "The way he conducts himself off the ice he's already miles ahead of a lot of rookies in the league, as far as his composure and maturity level go. Just the way he handles himself ... No one doubts that he's going to be a dominant player in the league and the cornerstone of this franchise."

Jody Shelley, the Blue Jackets' 27-year-old tough guy and one of Nash's closest teammates, is also impressed. Shelley says Nash is mixing well with players who are married and have kids even though he wasn't even the oldest player on the junior team he came from. The age gap does limit what Nash can do socially with his teammates, however, because he isn't old enough to go to bars. "The social scene is go to movies, play PlayStation, we go to dinner all the time, go to the mall and go shopping," Shelley says. "But he's ready for the NHL. He's so mature beyond 18, things don't seem to bother him. He's just here and he does his job and he plays hockey and it's going well." HYS

BRAD RICHARDS #19

TAMPA BAY LIGHTNING • CENTRE

Height: 6-1 Weight: 194 Born: May 02, 1980 – Murray Harbour, PEI

Season	Team	GP	G	A	TP	PIM	+/-	Shots	Pct
2000–2001	Lightning	82	21	41	62	14	-10	179	11.73
2001–2002	Lightning	82	20	42	62	13	-18	251	7.96
2002–2003	Lightning	80	17	57	74	24	3	277	6.13
NHL Totals		244	58	140	198	51	-25	707	8.20

For the first few mornings he woke up in tears, thousands of miles from home, in a strange bed and a strange province, feeling so homesick he could barely stand to get up. He missed his family and his friends. He missed Prince Edward Island and the tiny fishing village of Murray Harbour where he had lived since he was a baby — until now, that is. Suddenly, 14-year-old Brad Richards was alone in another world, at a boarding school in south Saskatchewan. It wasn't an easy adjustment.

"It was very difficult at the start," Richards says about his bold move as a young teenager to Athol Murray College of Notre Dame. "I was waking up every morning crying. It just didn't seem right waking up and you're not at your parents' house."

Leaving home at such a tender age was one of the sacrifices Richards made for hockey. In the end, it was probably the most important move of his young life, setting him on the road to his current career in the NHL.

But at the time it was difficult for Richards and his dad, Glen, to be sure they were doing the right thing. Notre Dame offered Brad a chance to play hockey at a high level and exposure to junior and college scouts. It offered him a chance to use his obvious knack for the game to further his education. But it was a long way from home.

"I found it awful, awful hard that first year," says Glen, a lobster fisherman in Murray Harbour. "I mean, a kid that young ... He and I had done everything together. It was just like losing your right arm to see him go."

While Glen and Delite Richards were sad to see their boy move away, they had no idea he was feeling so homesick. Glen says now that, had he been aware, he would have brought his only son home immediately. But Brad knew that Notre Dame was the best bet for his future, so he swallowed his sadness in silence.

"He never, ever said, 'I want to come home,' " Glen says now. "We didn't find out until the next year and by then the school had really grown on him."

It wasn't long at all before Brad grew to love Notre Dame, located in the town of

19
EASTON
EASTON

Wilcox, population 200, some 49 kilometres south of the provincial capital of Regina. He had a great hockey coach in Terry O'Malley and he soon hooked up with Vincent Lecavalier, who became his best friend.

Richards and Lecavalier met not long after each arrived at Notre Dame from homes far away from Wilcox, both geographically and culturally. Lecavalier comes from the Montreal suburb of Ile Bizard. The new friends roomed together at the boarding school, with Vincent taking the bottom bunk and Brad the top. Some nights they would talk about their NHL dreams, occasionally speculating how great it would be if they could play in hockey's big leagues together. One day, years later, those dreams would come true.

For Brad Richards the hockey dream started much earlier than at Notre Dame, however. His dad took him skating at the local arena in Murray Harbour when he was just 2 1/2. "He stepped onto the ice and just kind of took off," Glen says. "Brad took right to it. He was always wanting to go to the rink, and when the time was over he never wanted to get off."

Glen Richards had played a little competitive hockey himself, tending goal up to the junior A level in P.E.I., with both King's County and Charlottetown. He coached Brad through the minor-hockey ranks, too, but says he gently steered his son away from the crease.

Brad remembers it a little differently. "I wanted to be a goalie, like him. He wouldn't let me. He said it was the worst position. He always said you can't win playing goal: If anything goes wrong, it's your fault."

Instead, Brad played defence, where his skating ability and gift for seeing the ice helped him become one of Prince Edward Island's best minor-hockey players and allowed him to successfully play ahead of his age group. As he grew older he moved up to play forward, where his passing ability enabled him to pile up the points.

Although Canada's island province isn't known as a hotbed of professional puck prospects, Richards says that growing up in Murray Harbour — one of a cluster of fishing villages about 35 minutes east of Charlottetown on the eastern shore of Prince Edward Island — had its advantages.

"P.E.I. is not overly populated," says Richards, whose hometown has only about 350 residents. "We got tons of ice time as kids — we were always practising. And usually there were only 10 or 11 players on the hockey teams I played on, so we got lots of ice time."

Richards and his family heard about Notre Dame, a private Catholic boarding school, through Allen Andrews, who operates a well-known hockey school in P.E.I. Andrews knew Notre Dame coach O'Malley and helped make the arrangements for Brad to go there. As well as offering good hockey, good schooling and a chance to get on the college hockey scouts' radar it was also a chance for Brad to pursue something other than lobster fishing, a trade at which his father, grandfather and great-grandfather had each made his living. "It never really grasped Brad," Glen says of lobster fishing. "It can be pretty dirty days. When it's nice out on the boat, there's nowhere else you'd rather be, but when it's not ..."

ROCKET MAN

Brad Richards had to leave home to play major junior hockey, but now young Prince Edward Island players have another option. Richards is among a group of 40 owners of the P.E.I. Rocket, a team that began playing in the QMJHL in 2003. "It's a great step for the island to see the future NHL players," Richards told the Canadian Press. "There will be NHL scouts coming into town, there will be chances to host Memorial Cups, seeing young players turn into NHLers. They are all playing for a reason at that age."

"It was never really in my blood," Brad says. "I never really wanted to go out. It was something I didn't want to do and he didn't want me to do, either. It's a tough life."

Glen and Delite wanted their boy to get an education and have choices. "It was hard to let him go to Notre Dame," Glen says. "But it was to advance his hockey and, at the same time, get his schooling, too."

The move turned out to be a great one for Richards, who would spend three years at the Saskatchewan school. But coach O'Malley's first impression of the newcomer from P.E.I. was that, at about five foot six, he was pretty small.

"I wondered if he was going to make it," says O'Malley, a member of the International Ice Hockey Hall of Fame and now president of the school. "But Brad saw the ice very well.

"P.E.I. IS NOT overly populated. We got tons of ice time as kids—we were always practising. And usually there were only 10 or 11 players on the hockey teams I played on ..."—Brad Richards

He was certainly tough enough and smart enough, but I was concerned about his size."

The coach needn't have worried. Richards starred for two seasons with the Hounds bantam team, scoring at a point-a-game clip, sometimes playing with Lecavalier and sometimes even taking shifts on defence. "He was very mobile, saw the ice and was a tremendous passer," O'Malley recalls. "He was the point man on the power play."

Lecavalier and Richards were the only two grade 9 students at Notre Dame to make the school's bantam team and they quickly developed a bond. For Richards, the experience at the school was a major factor in his development. "Not too many people get that kind of coaching at that age," he says. "And we had to mature so quickly being away from home. We had to fend for ourselves so much sooner. We grew as people."

Like Lecavalier, Richards was called up to the Notre Dame midget team for the playoffs during his first two years. After his best friend left for the Quebec Major Junior Hockey League, Brad starred for the Hounds' entry in the Saskatchewan Junior Hockey League, even though he was only first-year midget age. Richards posted 39 goals and 87 points and captured SJHL rookie-of-the-year honours.

Although Richards' goal had been to land a college scholarship, he followed the lead of his buddy Lecavalier in his next step up the hockey ladder. Lecavalier had gone on to play for the Rimouski Oceanic, in a town of about 50,000 in Quebec's St. Lawrence River Valley. The Oceanic had noticed Richards' name on a scouting list a few months later and asked Lecavalier if he knew the Notre Dame prospect. By the next season Richards was in Rimouski, too. As a rookie in his NHL draft year, he posted an impressive 33 goals and 82 assists.

Those numbers were enough to make him a top prospect heading into the NHL entry draft in Buffalo. A handful of family members attended the event and watched as Brad was selected 64th overall by the Tampa Bay Lightning on the same day his friend, Vincent Lecavalier, went No. 1 overall to the same club.

While Lecavalier jumped straight into the NHL as an 18-year-old, Brad returned to the QMJHL, where he continued to develop and post some astonishing numbers. In his second season with the Oceanic, he turned in a 131-point campaign that included 92 assists over just 59 games. But the best was yet to come in his third major junior season: He amassed 71 goals and 115 assists in 63 games to earn Quebec and Canadian player-of-the-year honours.

The postseason was the sweetest, however. Richards was named the Memorial Cup MVP after he led the Oceanic to the Canadian major junior championship in the Halifax Metro Centre to cap his final season with Rimouski in grand fashion.

His parents and younger sister, Paige, enjoyed the fact that Rimouski was just a 7 1/2-hour drive from Murray Harbour, and the Oceanic also travelled to the Maritimes to play other QMJHL teams. "We went back and forth a lot," Glen Richards says. "The 7 1/2 hours seemed like it was next door after having him in Saskatchewan for three years."

Richards broke into the NHL the next year, joining Lecavalier in the Lightning lineup to complete the dream they had shared as 14-year-olds at Notre Dame. He made his mark right away, posting 21 goals and 41 assists in 82 games to make the NHL All-Rookie team. He also finished second to San Jose Sharks' goalie Evgeni Nabokov in rookie-of-the-year voting.

Richards followed that up with an identical 62-point season as a sophomore before cranking up the numbers in his third season. In 2002–3, he finished with 17 goals along with career bests of 57 assists and 74 points to place among the NHL's top 25 scorers and help Tampa Bay to the Southeast Division title. He added five assists in 11 playoff games before Tampa Bay was eliminated by the New Jersey Devils in the second round.

"It's just having another year in the league," Richards says when asked what the secret was in his third NHL season. "And on our team, the top four or five guys are all having career years. That makes a difference."

Becoming an impact player in the NHL, helping the Lightning into the playoffs for only the second time in franchise history and being able to do that alongside his longtime friend adds up to a storybook script.

"It is surreal sometimes," Richards admits. "It seems like forever ago since we met because we've been through so much together. Some days, we just look at each other and shake our heads that this has all happened."

Glen Richards says it doesn't seem that long ago that Brad was just a little guy skating on the ponds around Murray Harbour. "Going to Notre Dame was probably the move that got everything going," says the proud father. "Looking back, it was definitely the right thing to do. I always come back to the sacrifices Brad made. He was so strong. He could have called us and said, 'I want to come home.' I'm sure he thought about that. He left friends and family and everything behind. But he always had a goal in his mind."

JOFA

DANIEL & HENRIK SEDIN #22 | #33

DANIEL SEDIN • VANCOUVER CANUCKS • LEFT WING

Height: 6-1 Weight: 190 Born: September 26, 1980 — Ornskoldsvik, Sweden

Season	Team	GP	G	A	TP	PIM	+/-	Shots	Pct
2000–2001	Canucks	75	20	14	34	24	-3	127	15.74
2001–2002	Canucks	79	9	23	32	32	1	117	7.69
2002–2003	Canucks	79	14	17	31	34	8	134	10.44
NHL Totals		233	43	54	97	90	6	378	11.37

HENRIK SEDIN • VANCOUVER CANUCKS • CENTRE

Height: 6-2 Weight: 192 Born: September 26, 1980 — Ornskoldsvik, Sweden

Season	Team	GP	G	A	TP	PIM	+/-	Shots	Pct
2000–2001	Canucks	82	9	20	29	38	-2	98	9.18
2001–2002	Canucks	82	16	20	36	36	9	78	20.51
2002–2003	Canucks	78	8	31	39	38	9	81	9.87
NHL Totals		242	33	71	104	112	16	257	12.84

Vancouver newspaper reports described it as "The Miracle at the Fleet Center" and "a mind-blowing deal that could shape this team's destiny for the next 10 years."

It was June 26, 1999, and the Vancouver Canucks had just pulled off some major horse-trading at the NHL draft table in Boston. General manager Brian Burke had swung a deal that enabled his club to draft twin Swedish sensations Daniel and Henrik Sedin at Nos. 2 and 3 overall, respectively. Back home in Vancouver, long-suffering hockey fans were abuzz about a couple of players being billed by some as "Twin Forsbergs."

Fast forward a few years and that level of hype now seems almost foolish. The Sedin twins have proved to be competent, capable NHL players, but they haven't come close to matching the level of Colorado Avalanche superstar Peter Forsberg. In fact, some fans would now even describe them as twin disappointments.

But hold on a minute. While it's true the Sedin twins haven't exactly set the NHL on fire during three seasons with the Canucks, that doesn't mean they won't eventually put up the sorts of numbers that were projected when they were the red-headed darlings of draft day back in 1999.

Rangy Daniel and Henrik Sedin hail from Ornskoldsvik, a mill city of about 257,000 people that sits on the Gulf of Bothia in the northern half of Sweden. It's the same hockey-crazy city that produced Forsberg and Canucks scoring star Markus Naslund, as well as former Vancouver standout Thomas Gradin.

SEEING DOUBLE
For former Vancouver Canucks winger Trent Klatt, playing on a line with identical twins Daniel and Henrik Sedin sometimes posed a bit of a problem. "The hardest part was, you get back to the bench and you want to talk about a play that happened. Obviously, in the dressing room, I could look at them and tell them apart. But I'd have a hard time, when it's that quick on the ice, knowing which one was which."

Naslund, who has surpassed the 40-goal mark for the past three seasons, scored only four times in 71 games during his rookie NHL campaign with the Pittsburgh Penguins in 1993-94. He had only 11 points that year as a 20-year- old, the same age the Sedin twins were when they made the jump to the NHL.

Naslund, in fact, didn't start producing big offensive numbers until his sixth NHL season, when he piled up 66 points for the Canucks. And it isn't just foreign standouts who sometimes take a while to adjust to hockey's finest league: One of the Canucks' other major stars — aggressive power forward Todd Bertuzzi out of Sudbury, Ontario — didn't hit his stride as an NHL force until his fifth season.

The bottom line is the Sedins didn't turn 23 until well into their fourth training camp with the Canucks. They are still chronologically young as NHL players and there are still sound reasons to think there will be significant improvement.

"Coming into this league, obviously, there were very high expectations for them," says 12-year NHL veteran and former Canucks' linemate Trent Klatt. "It's not very easy living up to those expectations, though. They're doing a good job adjusting. They're improving every year, I think."

Not quickly enough for some, however. The most elementary way to rate any forward's performance is by points, and many don't believe the Sedins have delivered on the promise of their lofty draft status. Daniel, who was supposed to be the scoring winger of the pair, had a promising 20-goal, 14-assist rookie season. But he notched only nine goals in a 32-point season as a second-year NHLer, prompting some criticism from Vancouver's ever-watchful hockey media. In Year 3, things got worse: He was a healthy scratch for the Canucks three times and went through a span of 16 games when he scored just once. Daniel finished the season with a disappointing 14 goals and 17 assists while going plus-8.

Henrik, a playmaking centre, has consistently produced better numbers. After a 29-point rookie season that included nine goals, he had 16 goals and 20 assists in his second year. In 2002–3 he posted his best season as an NHLer, accumulating eight goals and 31 assists and going plus-9.

The Sedins made much more of an impact in the 2002–3 playoffs. They were two of the most effective postseason performers for the Canucks, who were upset by the Minnesota Wild in a seven-game second-round series. Daniel finished with six points and Henrik five in the team's 14-game playoff run.

The twins themselves admit to being unhappy with their regular-season production, but they also realize that expectations are not always easy to live up to. When asked if too much was expected when they were drafted, the twins not surprisingly have similar answers.

"There are always expectations when you get drafted high," Daniel says, "We each knew it was going to be tough for the first two years. It doesn't bother us too much. We have a lot of pressure that we put on ourselves. We don't worry about what the media says."

"I don't know," Henrik says, shaking his head slowly and considering the question carefully. "The media's always putting expectations on us, really since we were just coming up in Sweden and starting to play for the big team there. That hasn't really bothered us too much. But I think people who didn't realize how young we were [when they first went to Vancouver] or don't follow hockey that closely, they read the papers and thought we were, I guess, [going to be] unbelievably good. But it's tough to come over and play in this league and there's a lot of good players, so ... I think the people who know hockey, they know that we're still young."

Of the twins, Daniel is the youngest. Their mother, Tora, gave birth to Henrik about six minutes before Daniel on September 26, 1980. The twins first learned to skate at age five, following the path of their older brothers, Peter and Stefan, as they grew up in Ornskoldsvik, a town in which just about every boy dreams of being a hockey player.

Their father, Tommy, a school principal, coached their older brothers in the game. "We were around the rink the whole time watching them," Henrik recalls, "so it was pretty easy for us to start with hockey."

"Hockey is the biggest sport where we're from — and soccer, too," says Henrik, who like his brother was a midfielder in the grass game. "Soccer isn't really as big a deal when you're growing up there, though, because it's a long winter for us, so you can't really get a good soccer team up there."

The twins began playing organized hockey around age seven but they weren't immediately stars. "We weren't very good," recalls Daniel. "We were just decent hockey players." They didn't immediately play for the biggest club in their city, run by mill company MoDo. Instead they played for Jaovee, a smaller organization with an outdoor rink, and the players often had to help clear the snow from the ice surface before they could skate. "It was a good club to start out with," Daniel says.

It also worked to the advantage of the twins' development. By age 11 they were playing regularly with older players. "The club didn't really have [enough] kids to fill out all their ages, so they had to put different ages together," Henrik recalls. "So we played with the guys who were two years older all the time ... I think that was really important for us."

It helped by the time the twins jumped to MoDo, the largest program in their city and the same club that had produced Naslund, Forsberg and Gradin. MoDo also put the Sedins with older players and by the time they were 17 they were playing with the organization's top team in the Swedish elite league. "I think everybody grows up wanting to make that MoDo team," Daniel says.

It wasn't until then, however, that the Sedins began thinking seriously about a professional future in the game. "We played for fun. I didn't have any goals about making the NHL," Daniel says. "When we made the elite league with MoDo as 17-year-olds, we started thinking about the NHL."

The twins posted impressive numbers during their two full seasons playing against men in Sweden's top league, considered by some to be the second-best professional circuit in the world behind the NHL. Daniel recorded 42- and 45-point seasons while Henrik turned in 34- and 47-point efforts. As 18-year-olds, the Sedins were jointly named Swedish Elite League most valuable players.

That set the stage for their draft year, when scouts were touting them as two of the top young players in the world. But many observers thought they would be far more valuable together than they would be apart. The problem then for any NHL general manager hoping to land both was how to get the necessary draft picks in order to swing the deal.

Canucks boss Brian Burke managed to do just that, boldly throwing together a complicated set of deals to emerge on draft day with the No. 2 and 3 overall picks and a commitment from the Sedin family that the twins wanted to play in Vancouver.

> "WE HAVE A LOT of pressure that we put on ourselves. We don't worry about what the media says." —Daniel Sedin

While the Sedin selections received plenty of hype, the sobering reality for the struggling Canucks was that the twins would not come to the NHL right away. Daniel and Henrik opted to return for one final season in Sweden with MoDo, where they would finish high school and, hopefully, get physically ready for the tougher grind of the NHL.

When the Sedins did make the jump to the NHL, the Canucks actually met them halfway. The NHL team held its training camp for the 2000–1 season in Sweden, allowing the Sedins to be showcased at home with their new club.

Helping the twins make the adjustment to North America was the fact that they were accompanied to Vancouver by their girlfriends from Ornskoldsvik, Johanna with Henrik and Marinette with Daniel. "I think it's good to have someone who you can come home to after practice," Daniel says.

The Sedins say there wasn't much lifestyle adjustment necessary in Vancouver, especially with Markus Naslund and Mattias Ohlund already in the Canucks' lineup. "We had two Swedes here already and this city is fantastic," Henrik says. "The people are so nice, so it's very similar to Sweden in that way. Hockey-wise, though, you can't really relax any time out there on the ice. You've got to work hard every shift, otherwise they're going to hurt you. That was maybe the biggest adjustment."

Daniel believes the gruelling travel schedule is the biggest single difference in the NHL. When the twins played with MoDo, their longest flight was an hour and there was never a time change to deal with. It's much different in the NHL, of course, especially when playing in Vancouver requires more travel than playing on an eastern team. "It takes a physical toll," Daniel says.

JOFA
22
EASTON

The twins got off to a quick start once their first NHL regular season kicked in. Daniel had nine points and Henrik eight in their first 11 games, further fuelling the buzz about their futures in the league. When Daniel scored his first NHL goal, on October 8, 2000, in Tampa Bay, Henrik fittingly got the assist. Just over a week later the two combined for another goal by Daniel at home, with their parents in the General Motors Place crowd, and Henrik also notched his first NHL goal that night.

But in the ensuing seasons points have not come particularly easily for the Swedish pair. Daniel and Henrik Sedin have become effective two-way second-liners for their team, but they haven't produced a lot of offence. In their third season with the Canucks they began to take some heat for not providing the necessary supplementary scoring to the team's No. 1 line of Markus Naslund, Todd Bertuzzi and Brendan Morrison.

"Last year they took criticism, way too much criticism and it wasn't fair," says Canucks veteran Trevor Linden. "You know they're young players, but give them credit. Mentally they're very even-keeled guys. They don't get too up or down. They've handled it very well."

Canucks coach Marc Crawford has raised eyebrows by opting not to dress Daniel on a few occasions. He told reporters midway through Daniel's third season that the winger needed to play with more determination. But overall he offered a positive take on the twins.

"I think they're progressing very nicely," Crawford said. "They are important to the supplementary scoring for the team, but they do other things well ... There is no doubt that they are continuing to get better as they get stronger. [When they came here] I don't want to say they were pudgy but they were baby-faced. Now I think what you're seeing is that they're getting bigger and stronger."

While the media and some fans have at times been impatient, the Sedins' teammates remain supportive. The twins are seen as responsible defensive players who do other things well besides scoring and who are extremely effective at cycling the puck in the offensive zone.

"They're still physically not developed," Linden says. "They're young guys and they're big guys. They've got great attitudes. They're very intelligent players. They're only going to get stronger and faster as they mature. I'm talking when they're 25, when they've developed physically."

Although they have played mainly together since they arrived in Vancouver, the twins downplay any special connection they might have on the ice. In fact, they played on separate lines growing up in Sweden until they were thrown together permanently as 14- or 15-year-olds.

"I don't know if we play together well because we're twins," Daniel says. "I think it's because we've just played together for so long. If I played with someone else for that long, it would be the same way."

Klatt has nothing but good things to say about how the Sedins have handled themselves since coming to the NHL. "They're very quiet," he says. "They're very good young players. They keep to themselves. They speak when they're spoken to and they're not arrogant, they're not cocky, they're not flamboyant. They're very professional, they take care of themselves so that they're prepared to play every night."

One of the major questions surrounding the twins is whether they are fast enough on their skates to ever become first-line players or big scorers in the NHL.

"You know, every player's going to have something that someone's going to find fault with," Klatt says. "There are only a couple of players in the whole world who are perfect, right? So if quickness is one of [their faults], well, it's something that they can always work at. They're not afraid to go in the corners. They're not afraid to play the dirty game. They're not afraid to go in front of the net. They do all the things they need to do to be good hockey players."

Both twins believe that physical maturity will be a key to their improvement. They feel they are capable of putting up bigger numbers as they themselves get bigger. Daniel stands six foot one and Henrik six foot two — the older twin has always been a little taller — but each still weighs only about 200 pounds, making them slight for the heavy going in the NHL corners. "We can definitely get stronger. We're only 22 years old," Daniel says.

Henrik admits he and his brother aren't satisfied with what they've done so far as NHL players.

"Not really," he says. "We thought we were going to do better. But we're still young and we know that we can be much, much better in this league. It's going to take some years of hard work and hard practice, but we still think we can really make it over here." HYS

BAUER
19
EASTON

MARCO STURM #19

SAN JOSE SHARKS • LEFT WING

Height: 6-0 Weight: 195 Born: September 08, 1978 — Dingolfing, Germany

Season	Team	GP	G	A	TP	PIM	+/-	Shots	Pct
1997–1998	Sharks	74	10	20	30	40	-2	118	8.47
1998–1999	Sharks	78	16	22	38	52	7	140	11.43
1999–2000	Sharks	74	12	15	27	22	4	120	10
2000–2001	Sharks	81	14	18	32	28	9	153	9.15
2001–2002	Sharks	77	21	20	41	32	23	174	12.07
2002–2003	Sharks	82	28	20	48	16	9	208	13.46
NHL Totals		466	101	115	216	190	50	913	11.06

Most of today's NHL players grew up watching their heroes skate across the television screen, studying their trademark moves and later calling out their names while playing shinny and street hockey with their friends.

Marco Sturm isn't like most NHL players. He learned about the league's greats — names such as Yzerman, Kariya and Coffey — from a video game.

"I knew more about NHL players from PlayStation than from watching them on TV," Sturm chuckles now. "That's how I learned a lot of the players' names. Back then, there wasn't much hockey on German television."

When Sturm was a young boy, there wasn't much serious thought given to German-born-and-trained players skating in the NHL, either. Only towering six-foot-six defenceman Uwe Krupp of the Colorado Avalanche had come straight out of the European country to earn a regular place in North America's big leagues.

"By the time I was [junior age], I knew that I could play hockey for a living in Germany," Sturm says. "But nobody really thought I was going to play in the NHL."

He has managed to prove the doubters wrong. He jumped straight to the league as a 19-year-old, playing 74 games and collecting 30 points for the San Jose Sharks during the 1997–98 season. Before he had even reached age 25 he had already wrapped up his sixth season in the NHL.

Marco Sturm was born in Dingolfing, West Germany, in September 1978, more than 10 years before the fall of the Berlin Wall. His father, Johann, had played the game only recreationally, but he started Marco skating as a five-year-old and the youngster showed promise in hockey from the start, immediately becoming one of the best players on his team. He was a strong skater and a natural playmaker. "I always had many more assists than goals," he recalls.

A NEED FOR SPEED
Marco Sturm's German birthplace of Dingolfing is also home to a BMW automobile plant, where he worked for half a year before signing his first hockey contract. He likes speed off the ice as well as on it and has owned an impressive selection of sport and touring cars.

Sturm doesn't come from a particularly athletic family. Neither his father, his mother, Ingrid, nor his older sister, Nicole, were athletes. But Johann Sturm, a salesman in the computer industry, always encouraged his son to play hockey. "He kind of pushed me," Marco says.

As a boy, Marco also enjoyed soccer and tennis. In fact, he says that if he weren't a professional hockey player he would like to make his living on the soccer field. "I played everything 'til I was 14 or 15," he says. "Then I had to decide what I was going to do. I stuck with hockey. It was my best chance."

It was a good decision. Sturm became part of the club system in Landshut, a city of about 60,000 people in eastern Bavaria. He started with the club's junior team as a 14-year-old and made the move to the German elite league at 16, playing one game for Landshut that year. He earned a permanent spot playing against Germany's top men as a 17-year-old, becoming one of the youngest players to ever suit up in that country's elite league.

"It helped me a lot," Sturm says of the elite league, also known as the Deutsche Eishockey Liga, where he quickly had to get used to a faster, more physical brand of hockey in a quality circuit that includes a number of former NHLers such as Stephane Richer and Rene Corbet. North American fans might be skeptical about the calibre of play in foreign leagues, but Philadelphia Flyers coach Ken Hitchcock has described the DEL as being somewhere between the NHL and the American Hockey League. It obviously did the job for Marco Sturm, as well as drawing the attention of the European-based NHL scouts. After Sturm had posted 12 goals and 32 points as a 17-year-old, he had already turned enough heads to become a surprise first-round NHL selection in his draft year.

His father, Johann, and brother-in-law, Christian, both made the trip from Germany with Marco for the 1996 NHL draft in St. Louis. Marco had been advised that he was going to be selected, but he and his family were shocked when he went 21st overall in the first round to the Sharks. In doing so, he became the first German native ever selected in the first round.

"That was the biggest surprise," he says. "The draft was a thrill. I was really nervous. It was a different world for me. I knew that, suddenly, I was at another level."

Until he actually attended Sharks' training camp, however, Sturm wasn't certain whether he had what it took to play in the NHL. He didn't come to the NHL right away, returning to Landshut, where he recorded 16 goals and 43 points in his second elite-league season. It was then time to come to North America, but there were still no guarantees he could play at the NHL level despite his world, European and DEL experience.

"Before I came over, I was unsure," he admits. "I had no clue what the league was about. Then, when I did come here and went through a training camp, I kind of realized I might have a pretty good chance at playing here."

That much was evident by the time his first NHL season started and Sturm jumped out to a quick start, getting selected as the NHL's top rookie for November. He finished the season with a credible 30 points, including 10 goals, in 74 games and also played for Germany in the Winter Olympics tournament in Nagano, Japan.

His English wasn't good at the beginning. "I could understand more than I could talk," he recalls. "But the hockey English [words used on the ice], that I could understand."

Looking back on it now, Sturm feels his eventual command of English was probably sped up by the fact that he was alone in North America in that first year of playing with the Sharks. "I had to talk in English," he says. "I had no choice."

It was an adjustment coming from Europe to the U.S. "It was a big difference to come from a little country to one of the biggest," he once told fans in an NHL.com internet chat. "The language, the people, everything was a big change for me. There was nothing bad, it was just different. The players, the office people, everyone helped me a lot and made things easier."

Sturm's numbers have risen every NHL season and his reputation as a solid two-way forward has also grown. Not only has he collected between 30 and 40 points in each of his first five seasons, he has also posted a positive plus-minus rating in every year since his rookie campaign. He has shown versatility, playing either centre or left-wing, often on the Sharks' first or second line, and becoming known as a penalty-killing specialist. His skills were recognized in 1999 when he played in the NHL All-Star Game in Tampa, Florida.

In 2001–2, Sturm recorded a career-high 21 goals and 41 points and finished an impressive plus-23 for the season, setting a new Sharks franchise record for plus-minus. He followed that up with his finest season ever in 2002–3, with career bests of 28 goals, 48 points and 208 shots in 82 games.

"He has unbelievable wheels, and you've got to credit guys who come from a country where hockey is not the biggest thing," San Jose teammate Teemu Selanne told the Vancouver *Province* early in that 2002–3 season.

Sturm has settled nicely in the San Jose area, buying a home in Silicon Valley and enjoying tennis, golf and jet-skiing when he is not playing hockey.

Sturm has made some close friends on the Sharks, including Patrick Marleau, his roommate on the road. And although he certainly didn't grow up with the game, he has also become an American football fan since moving to the U.S., watching the 49ers and the Raiders and, like many Americans, finding himself looking forward to the odd Sunday in front of the television.

He has grown accustomed to the rigorous travel of the NHL, playing card games such as Texas Hold 'Em and other poker games on the team plane trips. At barely 25, he is already a seasoned veteran.

"I feel pretty good in the NHL now," he says. "I've got a lot more experience. I've played more than 400 games in the league already. Every hundred games, that's a big step."

If there is one area he'd like to improve, it's in finding the net more often. Sturm has had the luxury of playing with some fine offensive stars during his time with the Sharks, including Owen Nolan, Teemu Selanne and Patrick Marleau. He prefers to play centre, but when the Sharks use him at left wing he would like to be able to capitalize more consistently.

"Probably if there was one thing I have to work on it's to finish my chances," he says. "I get a lot of shots, a lot of good scoring chances, and sometimes I just can't bury it. Over here, it's tough to score."

Being able to carve a permanent place in the NHL and earn a very comfortable living playing his favourite sport has certainly been satisfying for Sturm. "Especially for me," he once told an NHL.com chat. "Being from Germany and to play in the NHL is a dream come true. That is a cool thing."

He still returns to Landshut every summer, where he's widely recognized as an NHL player. "The city's not that big and I played there before, too, so a lot of people know me," he says modestly.

"BY THE TIME I was [junior age], I knew that I could play hockey for a living in Germany. But nobody really thought I was going to play in the NHL." — Marco Sturm

Even more of his compatriots became familiar with his game when he played again for Germany in the 2002 Olympics at Salt Lake City, where he helped the team reach the quarter-finals.

One of his best hockey experiences came on a return to Germany in 2001, when his country hosted the world championship tournament. Sturm was Germany's leading scorer, finishing with four goals and five points in seven games to help lead his team into the medal round.

NHL players from Germany are becoming more common, although they are still relatively rare compared with players from more traditional European hockey powers and North America. A total of 32 German players have been drafted by NHL teams since 1969. Current Philadelphia Flyers defenceman Denis Seidenberg is a product of the German elite league, as is centre Jochen Hecht of the Buffalo Sabres, a teammate of Sturm's in Germany's Olympic lineup at Salt Lake City.

And Marco's own North American team made a point of using its first three selections of the 2001 NHL entry draft to select German prospects — centre Marcel Goc, defenceman Christian Ehrhoff and goaltender Dimitri Patzok. Goc went 20th overall in the first round to the Sharks, surpassing Sturm as the highest-drafted German player in NHL history.

Marco and Astrid, Sturm's girlfriend of four years from Landshut, were married in their native country during the summer of 2003. The couple will to return to Germany to live after Marco's NHL career is over. At least that's the plan now.

"You never know," Sturm says. "I'm still young. Hopefully, I'm going to play a lot of years over here."

JOE THORNTON #19

BOSTON BRUINS • CENTRE

Height: 6-4 Weight: 220 Born: July 02, 1979 — London, ON

Season	Team	GP	G	A	TP	PIM	+/-	Shots	Pct
1997–1998	Bruins	55	3	4	7	19	-6	33	9.09
1998–1999	Bruins	81	16	25	41	69	3	128	12.5
1999–2000	Bruins	81	23	37	60	82	-5	171	13.45
2000–2001	Bruins	72	37	34	71	107	-4	181	20.44
2001–2002	Bruins	66	22	46	68	127	7	152	14.47
2002–2003	Bruins	77	36	65	101	109	12	196	18.36
NHL Totals		432	137	211	348	513	7	861	15.91

With his team trailing by two goals late in an important playoff game, the lanky nine-year-old defenceman did something his coach with the St. Thomas, Ontario, novice rep team had never seen him do before. Young Joe Thornton took the puck and skated end-to-end, through most of the North London opposition, to score a goal. In fact, he did it twice, to provide his teammates with a lift right when they needed it most. And as the youngster with the curly blond hair skated back to the victorious bench, coach Brian Muscat asked the kid, "Joe, where did *that* come from?" The innocent reply emerged from behind a gigantic grin: "I really don't know, coach," he said.

"Honest to god, to this day, that's my best memory of Joe," says Muscat, who still lives and coaches hockey in St. Thomas.

It's a rather appropriate memory, too, because it demonstrates the manner in which Joe Thornton has consistently managed to rise to the top of the talent pool. That rise has taken him all the way from those novice days in St. Thomas to his current perch as captain and star of the Boston Bruins and one of the finest players in the NHL.

Back then, however, in the late '80s and early '90s, Thornton was a gangly kid in a city of 32,000 that is best known as home of the Ford Motor Company Crown Victoria automobile assembly plant. Thornton was actually born in nearby London, but the family moved south to St. Thomas when he was very young.

Joe was always the biggest kid on the St. Thomas minor-hockey teams coached by Muscat, who was Thornton's coach for five seasons, from the time he was eight until he was 12. "He was a big, gangly kid who never had to impose himself," recalls Muscat, now a high school teacher and hockey coach at Central Elgin in St. Thomas. "He was just bigger than all the other kids. In fact, he was a good foot taller than my son Matthew when they started playing together."

Joe was big, but he was coordinated, a rare combination. Though Thornton already stood five foot two as an eight-year-old and was an even six feet by the time he was 12, he always skated well and was good with the puck. Perhaps that wasn't surprising: His first cousin, Scott Thornton, preceded Joe into the NHL by seven years and has enjoyed a lengthy career in hockey's big leagues playing for Toronto, Edmonton, Montreal, Dallas and San Jose.

"Joe was always the best player on our teams," Muscat says. "Except we never made him have to think he was the best."

Muscat's philosophy with the rep teams at St. Thomas was to play all lines and players on essentially an equal basis. His teams had no power-play or penalty-killing units.

"YOU JUST COULD tell there was something special. The drive was always there. We never had to get on him about giving his best. Never, ever." —Brian Muscat, who coached Joe Thornton in minor hockey

Thornton got a little extra time on occasion by skating as a defenceman, but for the most part everybody shared the ice.

At the time, St. Thomas iced just one rep team in each age group. Muscat's crew, led by Thornton, did well, winning the Silver Stick championship emblematic of the North American title in both its novice and minor atom seasons.

Despite the equity on the ice, Muscat sensed there was something that separated Joe Thornton from the pack. He was big and talented, but there was also something unique inside the boy.

"You just could tell there was something special," the coach says. "The drive was always there. We never had to get on him about giving his best. Never, ever."

While Muscat tried not to put a lot of pressure on Thornton he did subtly motivate Joe, usually by mentioning the impressive talent level of the best player on the team St. Thomas was about to face. "Joe was always going to make sure he was going to play as well as that kid," says Muscat, once described by Thornton as the best hockey coach he ever had.

That competitiveness was likely fostered by the fact that Thornton's older brothers were athletic and bigger than he was and Joe always had to be ready to compete. That spirit wasn't restricted to hockey, either. Muscat remembers Thornton as a 10-year-old coming out for the rep baseball team he coached. Unlike the other hockey players, Thornton hadn't played on the travelling baseball team until then. "But by the end of the

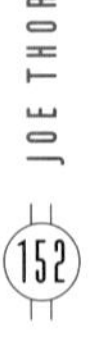

year he was the best player," Muscat says. The same went for basketball: In his first year of high school, Thornton went out for the team. Despite his height, he played guard and handled the ball. "By the end of the year, he was the dominant player," Muscat says.

All the other sports fell to the wayside, however, when Thornton entered the world of junior hockey and the game became a career path as well as a passion. After a brief call-up to the St. Thomas Stars of the Ontario junior B league as a 14-year-old, he joined the team full-time in the fall of 1994. As a 15-year-old, he amassed 40 goals and 64 assists in just 50 games with the Stars.

The Sault Ste. Marie Greyhounds of the Ontario Major Junior League subsequently made Thornton the No. 2 pick in the league's annual bantam-age draft. Joe Paterson, the Greyhounds' coach at the time, remembers the team's scouts being delighted when the Sarnia Sting passed on Thornton with the No. 1 pick. For Joe Thornton, going to Sault Ste. Marie was a chance to follow in the footsteps of his boyhood hockey idol, Wayne Gretzky, who had also played junior for the Greyhounds.

"He was big for a 16-year-old," says Paterson, who coached Thornton during both his seasons with the Greyhounds. "And you could just see he had great instincts for the game."

Paterson, now an assistant coach with the American Hockey League's Hamilton Bulldogs, remembers Thornton, even at 16, as a player who had great vision and saw the ice well. The kid could also score and he had tremendous size. "He was gritty, too."

Joe jumped in and contributed immediately at the major junior level on a talented team that included future Vancouver Canucks starting goaltender Dan Cloutier. In his first season with the Greyhounds, Thornton piled up 76 points in 66 games. He didn't shy away from the rough stuff, accumulating 53 minutes in penalties. For his efforts, he was named OHL and Canadian major junior rookie of the year.

"He had to play against players 17, 18, 19 and even the overage players teams had," Paterson says. "It was a huge jump for a 16-year-old but he jumped in right away. He wasn't intimidated. He even fought his first year."

Paterson remembers opponents going after the big rookie, trying to throw him off his game. That didn't seem to faze him. In fact, during the playoffs Thornton fought 19-year-old Sean Brown of the Sarnia Sting, a noted OHL tough guy who years later would become his NHL teammate with the Bruins.

If Joe Thornton created a spark in the OHL as a 16-year-old, he absolutely set the league on fire during his second season with the Greyhounds, which also happened to be his NHL draft year. Over just 59 games, the tall centre with the eye-opening passing skills racked up 41 goals, 81 assists and 123 penalty minutes. He added 19 points and 24 penalty minutes during 11 postseason games.

"In comparison to a lot of other players, if he continued to grow the potential was unlimited," Paterson says. "He had all the ingredients and he had the work ethic."

Those qualities made Joe the consensus No. 1 pick heading into the 1997 NHL entry draft

CCM
CCM
CCM
VECTOR

in Pittsburgh. As that draft approached, the focus intensified on the lanky kid with the blond locks and the rugged good looks.

During the final year of his amateur career, Thornton became the player to watch in Canadian junior hockey. He was already well known by the hockey media, the youngest member of Canada's gold-medal-winning team at the 1997 world junior championships in Geneva and ranked No. 1 overall by NHL Central Scouting.

"Other [OHL] teams we played on the road would use Joe as a selling point for games," Paterson says. "There was a lot of pressure, but he never really looked at it that way. It always seemed he knew how to have fun playing the game."

There were no surprises in June's entry draft as Thornton went first overall to the Boston Bruins, ahead of No. 2 Patrick Marleau and third pick Olli Jokinen. With their second pick in that draft, No. 8 overall, Boston made another key choice, selecting Russian forward Sergei Samsonov.

Much was expected of the teenage Thornton by the time he hit Boston, where the Bruins had finished dead last in the entire NHL with just 61 points the previous season.

ONE BIG FAMILY

At six foot four and 225 pounds, Joe Thornton is considered big by pro hockey standards and his physical dimensions are certainly a factor in his game. But he is actually the smallest and youngest of three Thornton brothers. Al, the oldest sibling, stands six foot five and John, the middle boy, is six foot six. Their mother, Mary, is nearly six feet tall and their father, Wayne, stands six foot one.

Following the draft, Thornton, wearing a Boston sweater, was the cover-boy for *The Hockey News*. And expectations only grew as Bruins coach Pat Burns decided to keep the 18-year-old in the NHL rather than ship him back to junior. But, perhaps predictably, the transition to hockey's best league was difficult. In his rookie season, while the teenager billeted with a family arranged through the Bruins and finished high school by correspondence, Joe struggled on the ice for the first time in his life.

Not helping was the fact that the big rookie's playing time was severely limited by Burns, who tried to ease Thornton into the NHL. He appeared in only 55 games, scoring just three goals and adding four assists.

The Bruins made the playoffs that season, finishing second in the Northeast Division to surprise most observers. But many fans who hoped Thornton might make an instant impact were disappointed with his rookie results, particularly when they were compared with those of Samsonov. The Russian, who was only a year older, had managed to pile up 22 goals and 47 points while capturing NHL rookie-of-the-year honours.

"Any 17- or 18-year-old kid coming into a professional locker room, it's a little intimidating," Thornton recalled during an interview with NHL.com columnist Larry Wigge. "Nobody can really tell you what to expect. You've just got to learn it yourself. It's a sink-or-swim mentality."

Paterson believes staying with the Bruins at such a young age was ultimately good for Thornton. "But there's a big difference in strength and adjustment when a young player like that goes to the NHL," he says.

Year 2 in the NHL was much more encouraging. Already bigger and stronger than he had been as a rookie, Joe played in 81 games, averaged more than 15 minutes of ice time and compiled 41 points, including 16 goals.

Thornton's ice time and production levels jumped radically in his third and four years in the NHL as he matured and grew more comfortable with the pro routine. Averaging more than 21 minutes a game, he had 60 points in his third season and a career-best 71 in his fourth, when new, hard-nosed Bruins head coach Mike Keenan seemed to make particular strides in helping the big centre develop his game.

"I won't say I wasn't disappointed that I wasn't playing more and producing more in my first two seasons," Thornton later told NHL.com. "I wondered why I was still playing on the second and third lines in my third season. But I realized they wanted me to earn my ice time. Burnsie [coach Pat Burns] made me watch the game and learn. Then Mike Keenan came in and he forced me to grow up and be a man.

"I think I can look back now and say I became more mentally tough, especially when Mike came in during my fourth season. He pushed and prodded me — asked me if I wanted to be the player I was capable of, or just another one of those guys who, years from now, was considered a player who had the potential ... but couldn't take advantage of it."

One of the factors in fulfilling his vast potential was developing the physical edge to his game and using his size effectively to create space and become one of the premier power forwards in the league. It's probably no coincidence that Thornton racked up 107 penalty minutes in his fourth NHL season and then added 127 penalty minutes in his fifth.

Thornton's development was enough to prompt Bruins coach Robbie Ftorek to name him as the team's captain just prior to the 2002–3 season, replacing Jason Allison, who had been traded to the Los Angeles Kings the previous October. At age 23, Thornton was at the time the NHL's youngest player to wear the "C" on his sweater.

The best was certainly yet to come, however. Joe Thornton put it all together during his sixth NHL season. In the process he jumped to another level, moving from promising youngster to certified star.

He posted his first 100-plus point season, finishing with 101 points, including career-best totals of 65 assists and 196 shots over 77 games. His efforts left him third in the NHL scoring race, five points behind winner Peter Forsberg of the Colorado Avalanche and three behind runner-up Markus Naslund of the Vancouver Canucks. Thornton also finished with 109 penalty minutes and a career-best plus-12 rating for the season as he led the Bruins to a playoff spot.

"I always believed he had the potential to lead the league in scoring," says Joe Paterson, Thornton's former junior coach. "He was pretty darn close to doing that this year."

Although he opted not to join the 2003 Canadian world championship team, Thornton is thought to be a player around whom Canada will build its 2004 World Cup and 2006 Olympic teams. One of his biggest hockey disappointments was not making the Team Canada lineup for its gold-medal run through the Salt Lake City Olympics in 2002. But his international moment on the rink will no doubt come, as will, many predict, future Hart trophies and NHL scoring titles. After all, he completed his sixth NHL season before he had reached his 24th birthday.

"That whole No. 1 [draft] pick thing was totally blown out of proportion," Thornton reflected for NHL.com. "No. 1 overall is just a number. A nice number, but just a number nonetheless. Look around at the greatest players in the game and the evolution of a top prospect happens quickly for a chosen few such as Bobby Orr, Wayne Gretzky and Mario Lemieux. The rest of us have a lot of growing up to do."

Joe Thornton has certainly grown into one of the game's bright young superstars, just as Brian Muscat always knew he would. The St. Thomas coach still keeps in touch with the player who amazed him all those years ago by going end-to-end to lift his team in that unforgettable novice playoff game.

"That's a trait I've always seen in Joe," Muscat says. "No matter what level he's at, he'll rise to show that he's the best player there."

PHOTO CREDITS

All photos by Bruce Bennett Studios: Claus Andersen, 154; Bruce Bennett, 14, 51; Dave Kaye, 143; Jim Leary, 54, 70, 84, 126; Scott Levy, 89, 131, 134; Jim McIsaac, 16, 18, 22, 34, 42, 43, 66, 72, 79, 93, 96, 107, 110, 119, 138 (bottom), 146; Dale MacMillan, 28, 46, 83, 118, 138 (top); Andy Marlin, 58; Lisa Meyer, 10, 122; Layne Murdoch, 28; Jason Pulver, 103; John Russell, 75, 98; Brian Winkler, 65, 155.

Cover: (from left) Joe Thornton, Boston Bruins (Brian Winkler); Dany Heatley, Atlanta Thrashers (Brian Winkler); Jarome Iginla, Calgary Flames (Bruce Bennett).

ACKNOWLEDGEMENTS

The author would like to offer a special thanks to the following people: Associated Press hockey writer Kevin Woodley, for conducting several interviews that provided material and for consulting on player selection for this book; Derek Fairbridge, for his thoughtful editing of the manuscript and steering of this project; Michelle Benjamin, for her continued support as publisher of Raincoast Books; Chris Cuthbert, for agreeing to write the foreword to *Hockey's Young Superstars* and for consulting on selection of players; Genadi Boguslavski for interviewing Andrei Markov and providing background information; to all the National Hockey League teams who helped line up interviews and provided information; to all the parents, family members and coaches who generously gave valuable and entertaining insight into these young men; to all the players who took time out to be interviewed for this project; and to Lana, who put up with late nights and busy weekends.

The author would also like to thank the following people for their help in the creation of this book: Mark Awdycki, Paul Baxter, Red Berenson, Dan Bouwmeester, Frank Brewer, Bob Briere, Sylvie Briere, Chris Brumwell, T.C. Carling, Rick Carriere, Jeff Chynoweth, Hope Clark, Ian Clark, Bill Comrie, Ed Dempsey, Hayne Ellis, Scott Emmert, Russ Farwell, Pierre Gagne, Dave Griffiths, Peter Hanlon, Matt Hansen, Don Hay, Murray Heatley, Zack Hill, Ken Hodge, Dale Hunter, Steve Keogh, Steve Knowles, Rob Koch, Bruce Landon, Yvon Lecavalier, Terry O'Malley, Richard Martel, Denis Marleau, Jean Martineau, Terry Morris, Brian Muscat, Richard Nairn, Liz Nash, Brent Parker, Joe Paterson, Tim Pattyson, Mike Penny, Glen Richards, Liani Rosa, Dominick Saillant, Susan Schuchard, Todd Sharrock, Randy Sieminski, Warren Suitor, Tom Thompson, Trevor Timmins, Bill Tuele, Derek Van Diest, Karen Verzone, Rob Viccars, Jason Vogel and Don Waddell.

Information was gleaned from the following publications or services during the writing of this book: *Vancouver Sun*, *Province*, *Edmonton Journal*, *Edmonton Sun*, *Toronto Star*, *Toronto Sun*, *National Post*, *Globe and Mail*, *Ottawa Citizen*, *The Hockey News*, *Medicine Hat News*, *Canadian Press*, *Associated Press*, NHL.com, *Maclean's*, *Red Line Report*, *Atlanta Journal-Constitution*, *Montreal Gazette*, Faceoff.com, *Calgary Herald*, *Calgary Sun*, *San Francisco Examiner*, *San Francisco Chronicle*, *New York Post*, *National Hockey League Official Guide & Record Book*, *Miami Herald*, *Florida Sun-Sentinel*, *Les Canadiens* magazine, *Sports Illustrated*, *Palm Beach Post*, ESPN.com, *Windsor Star*, *Prince George Citizen*, *Cranbrook Daily Townsman*, *St. Paul Pioneer Press*, *Minneapolis Star Tribune*, CNNSI.com, *Hockey Digest*, *Victoria Times Colonist*, *Prospects Hockey* magazine, *Columbus Monthly*, *Columbus Dispatch*, HockeyZonePlus.com, TSN.ca, NHLPA.com, CBS Sportsline.com, jockbio.com and *PowerPlay* magazine.

ABOUT THE AUTHOR

Jeff Rud has worked as a sports writer for various Canadian newspapers for 22 years. He was both sports columnist and sports editor at the *Victoria Times Colonist*, and has covered the NHL for the *National Post*. He is currently a senior news reporter at the *Times Colonist*, specializing in education. Jeff's previous books include *Long Shot: Steve Nash's Journey to the NBA* and *Skywalking: How Ten Young Basketball Stars Soared to the Pros*. He lives in Victoria.